CANADA NORTH

Farley Mowat

CANADA NORTH

An Atlantic Monthly Press Book

Little, Brown and Company · BOSTON · TORONTO

© Copyright 1967
McClelland and Stewart Limited.

ATLANTIC–LITTLE, BROWN BOOKS
ARE PUBLISHED BY
LITTLE, BROWN AND COMPANY
IN ASSOCIATION WITH
THE ATLANTIC MONTHLY PRESS

PRINTED IN ITALY

Contents

Albums

PROLOGUE   *Myth and Reality*

Somewhere far to the north of Newfoundland, the St. Lawrence Seaway, Place Ville Marie, the Macdonald-Cartier Freeway, the bald-headed prairie and Stanley Park lies an unreal world conceived in the mind's eye, born out of fantasy and cauled in myth. It is a weird and terrible land where nothing is as it may seem. Home of the ice worm and the igloo, of mad trappers and mushing Mounties, of pingos and polar bears, of the legions of the damned that were conjured into being by Robert Service, its voice is the baleful whisper of the aurora borealis, the eerie howl of Jack London's malemutes and the whining dirge of C.B.C. wind machines. It is a "white hell", "the ultimate desolation", a "howling wasteland", "the Land that God Forgot" and "the Land God Gave to Cain". It is a region almost wholly of our contriving, and we have made of it so inimical a world that the truly alien moon, even as seen on television screens and in picture magazines, seems to have more reality.

This North, this Arctic of the mind, this frigid concept of a flat and formless void of ice and snow congealed beneath the impenetrable blackness of the polar night, is pure illusion. Behind it lies a lost world obscured in drifts of literary drivel, obliterated by blizzards of bravado and buried under an icy weight of obsessive misconceptions. The magnificent reality behind the myth has been consistently rejected by Canadians since the day of our national birth and is rejected still. Through almost a century the Far North has meant to Canadians either a nightmarish limbo or an oppressive polar presence looming darkly over southern Canada and breathing icily down our necks. During most of that century the handful of people who called themselves Canadians were engrossed in the occupation of the apparently limitless spaces on the southern fringes of the country. When that space was finally circumscribed and its limits reached, Canadians did not look northward to the challenge of the unknown half of their share of the continent. The northern myth seemed more than they could face, even as it had in the past. They shunned it then – they shun it still. With the exception of a very few outstanding individuals, most of them employed by the Geological Survey of Canada, the exploration of the High North was accomplished, not by Canadians, but by British, French, Scandinavian, German, American and even Portuguese adventurers – men who mastered the myth, faced the reality, and took their knowledge home with them to their native lands. Those who followed in the paths of the explorers and made use of their discoveries, the traders and merchant exploiters, were English, Scotch, French and American, and the companies that employed them (such as the

Hudson's Bay Company, Revillon Frères, Canalaska Trading Company) operated out of London, Paris, New York and Seattle. Even the missionaries, coming in time-honoured manner in the wake of trade, were aliens. Moravians from Germany, and Grenfell from England, worked the Labrador coast; throughout the rest of the North, Oblate priests from Belgium and France competed for souls with Anglican priests straight out from England. Meanwhile the seas of the Canadian North were being exploited by Scotch and American whalers. In the Yukon the placer gold fields were overrun by men of half a hundred lands – and there were precious few Canadians among them. White trappers, moving in on the Eskimos and Indians, were almost exclusively northern Europeans. Even Canada's standard-bearers of a token sovereignty in the Arctic, the North West (later the Royal Canadian) Mounted Police, got most of their first recruits from England, Scotland, Newfoundland and even farther afield.

The pattern is old and well established. A century after the nation's birth, about three-quarters of the exploration and exploitation of the Canadian North is being carried out by consortiums controlled by American, European and Japanese companies. Military occupation of the North, while nominally a joint undertaking, remains effectively American. Until the middle of the twentieth century almost the *only* Canadians in the Arctic were Indians and Eskimos; but they were people born to the reality and in any case were, and are, "Canadians" only by courtesy.

Only since the early 1950's have southern Canadians begun to glance over their shoulders northward. As yet only a handful have made the effort to penetrate to the reality behind the myth and to actually *go* north, not to make a quick buck and then flee south as if the very hounds of hell were on their heels, but to attempt to make themselves integral parts of a gigantic and exciting world spurned by the nation that pretends to own it.

They are very few indeed. Apart from government employees and similar transients employed by mines and military installations, there are not more than a few thousand Canadians of other than Eskimo or Indian ancestry living in a land that is larger than the ten provinces. And most of these few are concentrated in southern Yukon Territory and around Great Slave Lake. In the central and eastern reaches, themselves ten times as vast as Texas, only a few hundred southern Canadians make the North their abiding home.

These are the true pioneers in a nation that is fond of boasting about her pioneering spirit. Men like Bob Williamson at Rankin Inlet, Terry Ryan at Cape Dorset, Ross Peyton at Pangnirtung, Ernie Lyall at Spence Bay, Fred Ross at Cambridge Bay, Tom Butters at Inuvik, Allan Innis-Taylor at Dawson, Bob Engles at Yellowknife, Don Stuart at Hay River – these are of the few, the dedicated ones, who have committed their lives to a land the rest of us reject. They are trying desperately to neutralize the apathy and ignorance of southern Canada, to destroy the suffocating myth so that we others may come to know the North for what it really is. So that we may come to recognize it as a part of our nation.

Men like these believe that *la dolce vita* is the way of death for any country. They would have us face resolutely north to a world that offers us – if we are men and women enough to recognize and grasp the opportunity – not only the material wealth we crave, but a fighting chance of finding the greatness of spirit that Canada so signally lacks.

Canada North is a frank look at the reality behind the northern myth – a straight look at the land we have rejected.

Although historians give them little credit, much of the exploration of Canadian arctic waters was certainly lighted on its way by whalers. As early as 1520 Basque whalers were working Davis Strait. In 1719 the Dutch entered the game and the whaling rush was on. By 1722 there were 355 whaling ships of five nations (mostly Scots and English) 'fishing' in Davis Strait and Baffin Bay. The hazards were frightful. More than 500 whaling ships are known to have been lost in these waters alone, mostly caught and crushed in the ice. But the whalers went back time after time; one Scot, Peter Ramsay, died of old age in 1874 aboard the whaling ship Erik, while on his 56th consecutive annual voyage a-whaling in Baffin Bay.

THE FACE OF THE NORTH

Stretching across the upper reaches of this continent lies a primordial giant; one side rough-pelted by the dark taiga forests, the other naked under the white polar skies. This Titan-land is wrinkled by its own unimaginable antiquity, furrowed by ten thousand rivers, glittering with the Cyclopean eyes of its innumerable lakes. Its bones are the bones of an elder world—cold bones into which an eternal frost strikes deep. Its thin skin of tundra, lichened forest floor and palely gleaming water feels fleeting warmth from the summer sun. In many places, the skin is ruptured by mighty wounds which are the legacy of a glacial incubus a mile thick that implacably and irresistibly gouged into the fleshless ribs. The wounds have never healed. Remnants of the ancient ice-sheet still smother the heads and shoulders of great mountain ranges that rear out of the arctic seas to east and west. This is a world uncircumscribed, for it has no limits that the eye can reach. Seeming to stretch beyond all boundaries, this brooding Titan has many faces: some harshly brutal, some fantastically grotesque, some that are infinitely lovely.

At the top of the continent, the myriad serpentine channels of the Mackenzie Delta glitter at midnight.

The ebony scarp of Gibbs' Fiord rises sheer from the bone-chilling waters of Scott Inlet.

On Baffin Island, a river of ice, trapped between glowering cliffs, grinds toward the sea.

Near Southampton Island, in Hudson Bay, a series of elliptical islands poke their noses above the sea, creating a pattern like a modern abstract painting.

Drumlins, the clawmarks of the great ice sheet, score the face of the North. Enormous boulders gouged out these watery furrows and left island ridges as the glacier crawled across the pliant land.

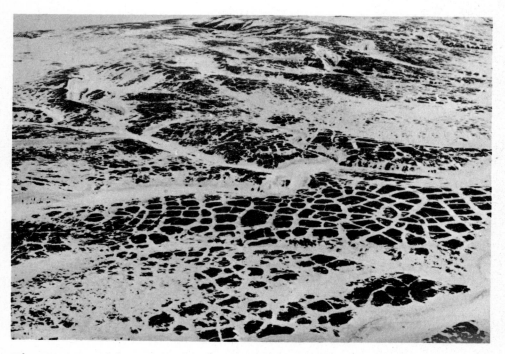

The action of frost cracks the tundra into strange polygon shapes.

The Labrador Iron Trough, from 20,000 feet up. It runs 600 miles, splitting the Ungava Peninsula.

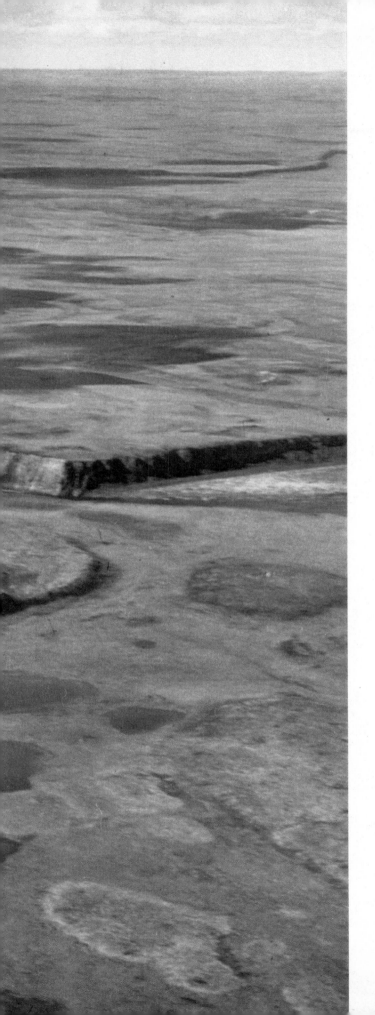

A giant frost boil, known as a pingo, rises 150 feet, above the Mackenzie Delta's frozen silt.

Coiling through the brilliant blues and greens of the Barren Grounds, the Coppermine River works its way to Coronation Gulf, in the Arctic.

*Like peaks sprouting from a dead planet, the saw-tooths
of the massive Mackenzie Mountains catch the sun's last rays.*

Deep lake and shallow pond, legacies from the vanished glaciers, splash vivid colour along the Teslin Valley.

*Forbidding as an ancient fortress, an iceberg wall
bars the head of Canyon Fiord, in central Ellesmere Island.*

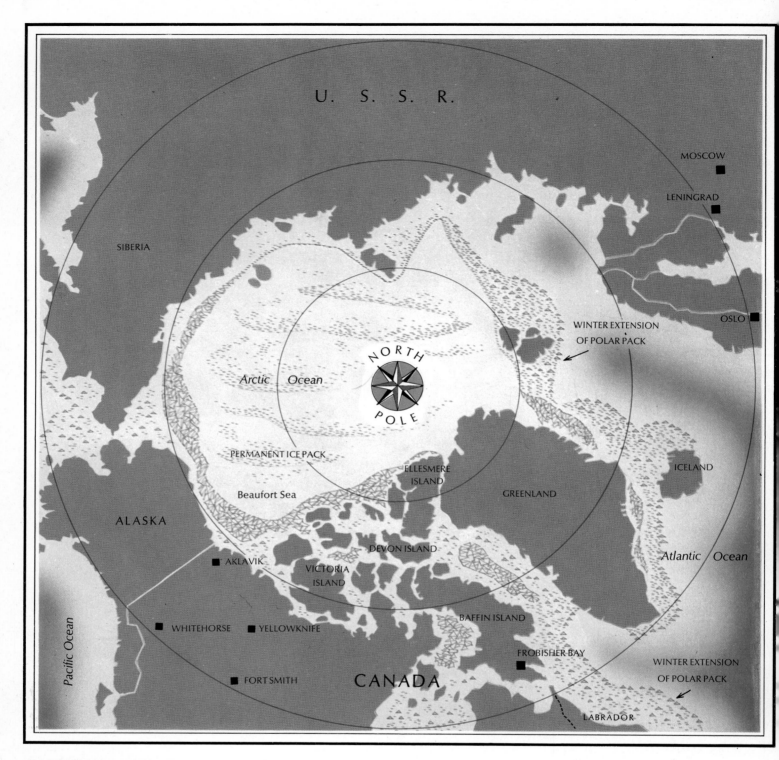

U. S. S. R.

MOSCOW

LENINGRAD

SIBERIA

OSLO

WINTER EXTENSION
OF POLAR PACK

Arctic   Ocean

NORTH
POLE

PERMANENT ICE PACK

ICELAND

ELLESMERE
ISLAND

Beaufort Sea

GREENLAND

ALASKA

Atlantic   Ocean

DEVON ISLAND

AKLAVIK

VICTORIA
ISLAND

BAFFIN ISLAND

Pacific Ocean

WHITEHORSE   YELLOWKNIFE

FROBISHER BAY

WINTER EXTENSION
OF POLAR PACK

FORT SMITH   CANADA

LABRADOR

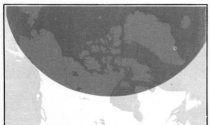

The Nature of the Beast I

The first difficulty that must be mastered in coming to grips with the Far North is to decide just where "north" begins and to ascertain its boundaries. Modern man has tried to evade the issue by separating the northern regions into sections, like a layer cake, so that he can deal with each part as a separate entity. Ask a scientist for a definition of "north" and you are instantly ears deep in boreal, subarctic and arctic zones, in isotherms, degree-days and permafrost limits. The truth is that the region has no arbitrary southern boundary except insofar as one exists in us as a state of mind. The situation is akin to that of an astronaut shot up in a rocket. At what point does he enter space? At no *point*, but only when he has become aware that he has entered an alien environment.

Since Canadians generally regard the Far North as an alien environment, they enter it when they leave their familiar world of the South behind them. The entry takes place in the upper reaches of the broad band of sombre coniferous forest that stretches across the entire breadth of Canada. Beginning near the Yukon – British Columbia border, this transition region slopes southeastward to Hudson Bay near Churchill where it swings sharply south paralleling the coast around James Bay. It then angles northeastward across Ungava to reach the Atlantic in the general vicinity of Nain on the Labrador coast. At its southernmost point (the top of James Bay) there are polar bears, seals, tundra and caribou, although the region is eight hundred miles south of the Arctic Circle. The North embraces the arctic zone but it is not limited to that region, nor to the Yukon and the Northwest Territories. It includes a sliver of northern Alberta, rather more of northern Saskatchewan, a goodly bite of northern Manitoba, a nibble of Ontario, a large part of Quebec, and the upper portion of Labrador.

It comprises a huge section of the earth's surface. Measuring from the north tip of Ellesmere Island (less than five hundred miles from the North Pole), the northern land mass strikes southward nearly two thousand miles to Cape Henrietta Maria on Hudson Bay – roughly the distance between Montreal and Calgary! And from the Alaska-Yukon border to Cape Dyer on the coast of Baffin Bay it stretches about the same distance east and west. It encompasses about one million, seven hundred thousand square miles – nearly half the total area of Canada.

The Canadian North reaches from Atlantic to Pacific but, more important, it extends almost to the heart of the Arctic Ocean. Canada *fronts* on this third ocean, which is a true mediterranean sea, in exactly the same way

Early whalers in arctic seas. An artist's impression; from Histoire des Peches, Paris, 1791

*"The Arctic displays as
much variety as
any other great natural
realm on earth"*

"Footprints" of hard snow are isolated by wind

Fantastic folded rocks in west wall of the Mackenzie Mountains.

Dredge tailings squirm over the Klondike flats.

A small lake in east Labrador is transformed into an icy palette.

Fractured ice makes a cool, crazy quilt.

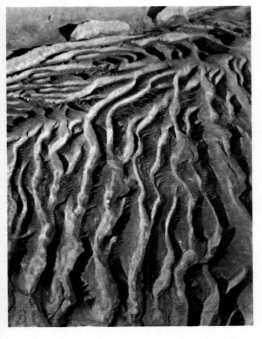

Erosion patterns mark north Ellesmere I.

that North Africa fronts on the European Mediterranean. This is a startling idea but one we would be well advised to get used to since Asia, Europe and North America all face each other across the almost land-locked polar sea and it is here that the three continents lie closest together. The orientation we get from looking at standard maps that show the North Pole at the top of beyond is arbitrary and wrong. This is *not* the way the world really is. The polar region is actually the *centre* of the northern hemisphere, and the geographic centre of Canada is in the Keewatin tundra 250 miles north-northwest of Churchill. Consequently when we turn our back on the North in the belief that there isn't much of interest in that direction, we are turning our backs on Europe and Asia, as well as on a great part of our own country. So far only the military men, preoccupied with death and destruction, have grasped this vital fact. When and if Canadians have the sense to appreciate its peaceful significance we may become a nation at the centre, instead of remaining a sycophantic satellite at the back door of the United States.

One of the particularly cockeyed misconceptions we have about our North is that it is all of a piece – or, at the most, of two pieces: a bleak expanse of frozen sea and a dreary wilderness of frozen plain. The truth is that the Arctic displays as much variety as any other great natural realm on earth. Stretching from central Labrador to Baffin Island, the up-tilted eastern edge of the Canadian Shield forms a shaggy range of glacier-encrusted mountains that are as formidable, as massively overwhelming in appearance, as anything in the Rockies. There is nothing to match them in eastern North America; yet they are almost unknown to us. They form the eastern wall of the North. Far to the westward, beyond the Mackenzie River, rise range after range of mountains that culminate in the St. Elias Range whose glacier-shrouded peaks soar to nearly twenty thousand feet in Canada and twenty-four thousand in Alaska. This is the western wall. Between these walls sprawls the worn and pitted face of the Canadian Shield composed of some of the oldest rocks on earth and so eroded by the work of the eons that only the time-smoothed stubs of its once-mighty mountains remain as undulating hills, giving relief to the naked, ancient rock. Here, in the Shield country, lies the greatest assemblage of lakes upon our planet. Between the western edge of the Shield and the risers of the Yukon Cordillera lies a broad tongue of lowlands that extends north from the Great Central Plains of North America, and down it one of the world's greatest rivers, the Mackenzie, carries the waters of the Peace, the Liard, and many lesser rivers to the Arctic Ocean.

North of the mainland lies the Arctic Archipelago, some nine hundred thousand square miles of lands constituting the largest island group in the world. These islands, too, have their variety. Some are mountainous, others are low and grassy plains, still others are bald stone and gravel deserts. Surrounding them lies a complex of sounds and channels as intricate as the most sophisticated maze.

Contained within the arctic lands of Canada is the vast inland sea of Hudson Bay in which the British Isles could be sunk without a trace. East of the main northern land mass a tremendous ice river carried on the Labrador Current flows down through Baffin Bay and Davis Strait, stretching an arctic tentacle as far south as Nova Scotia. The polar ocean is itself a species of "land", for it is perpetually ice covered and, though the ice moves, men can and do travel over it, and four-engine aircraft can land upon it.

Although the bone structure of most of the North, the Canadian Shield, is perhaps five million years old, much of the land looks raw and new. This is because a mere ten thousand years ago the entire region, except for the northwestern corner, lay buried beneath a gigantic ice sheet. The dome of the Keewatin District ice sheet was two miles thick. Its own titanic weight made the ice sheet plastic and it flowed implacably in all directions outwards from several high-domed centres. It scoured and gouged the ancient rocks, shearing off the surface soil layers and leaving behind an incredibly intricate pattern of water-filled valleys, basins, and deep coastal fiords. When the ice eventually melted it left the land littered with debris that ranged from barn-sized boulders to vast fields of shattered rock, and it embossed the naked bones of the country with a complex design of morainic ridges, drumlins, and long sinuous eskers of sand and gravel.

The ice had another, unseen effect. It deep-froze the rock beneath it, producing what we call permafrost. In the extreme northern islands permafrost penetrates fifteen hundred feet into the primeval rock. Even as far south as northern Manitoba the ancient frost remains, unyielding, only a few feet below the shallow surface layers that thaw in summer.

Remnants of the ice sheet itself also survive. In the wall of the eastern mountains some sixty thousand square miles of ice crown the heights and fill great valleys. Other remnants of ice persist in the mountains of the west.

Another generally held misconception about the North is that its climate is so hostile that only polar bears and Eskimos can endure it. Yet winter blizzards on the western prairies can match, in ferocity if not in intensity, the worst weather the North produces. Northern residents who have subsequently endured a winter at Saskatoon or Winnipeg have been heard to refer with nostalgia to the North as "the banana belt". Surprisingly, it is a dry world with very little rain or snowfall. Winter snows often lie deeper in Toronto or Montreal than in most parts of the North. Although not even the Yellowknife Chamber of Commerce would call northern winters balmy, they are as bearable as – if longer than – the winters at Ottawa, and the summers can be lovely. There are only two true seasons: winter and summer, the transitions between them being so brief as to be negligible. Near and north of the Arctic Circle the midsummer sun never sets and tempera-

It was still largely man vs. beast in Baffin Bay in mid 19th century.

tures sometimes persist in the comfortable sixties and higher for days on end. In winter above the Arctic Circle the sun vanishes for weeks or months, but this "long night" is seldom really dark. The Northern Lights often give a pervading luminosity and the glitter of the stars in a lucid atmosphere combined with bright moonlight provides enough light for almost all normal activity, including hunting.

The concept of the Far North as a lifeless land is another of our more grotesque illusions. Its southern fringes include the upper reaches of the taiga forests – mainly black and white spruce, larch, birch and poplar. The northward-marching trees of the taiga grow sparser and more stunted until they fade out in the vast open plains called tundra. There is no absolute line of demarcation between taiga and tundra – no real "timberline". The two regions interpenetrate like the clasped fingers of gigantic hands. There are pockets of tundra deep inside the forest, and oases of trees far out on the sweep of the tundra. Nor is the tundra all of a kind. There is alpine tundra high on mountain slopes, shrub tundra close to the taiga region, sedge tundra to the north, moss-and-lichen tundra still farther north and, on the extreme northern islands, fell-field tundra where vegetation finally gives up its stubborn attempt to occupy the remote lands that lie surrounded by unyielding polar ice. But in summertime most tundra regions boast an array of flowering plants of infinite number and delight. Although they are small, they mass in such profusion that they suffuse hundreds of square miles with shifting colour. They form a Lilliputian jungle where hunting spiders, bumblebees, small and delicate moths and butterflies abound. Black flies and mosquitoes abound too, alas, and there is no evading the fact that they are the bane of summer in the North.

Birds breed almost everywhere. Mammals of many species, ranging from squat, rotund lemmings to massive muskox occupy the lands. The seas are home to whales, seals, obese walrus and sinuous white bears. The seas are also rich in fishes as are the numberless inland lakes. For those with eyes to see, the North is vitally and vividly alive. Long, long ago, men of other races out of another time recognized this truth and learned to call the northern regions "home".

Man did not always win. A French artist depicts a tragedy on the ice.

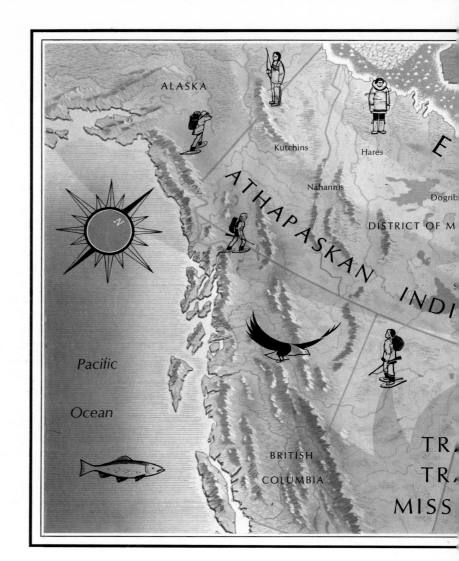

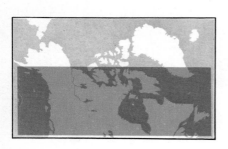

2

The Northern Blood

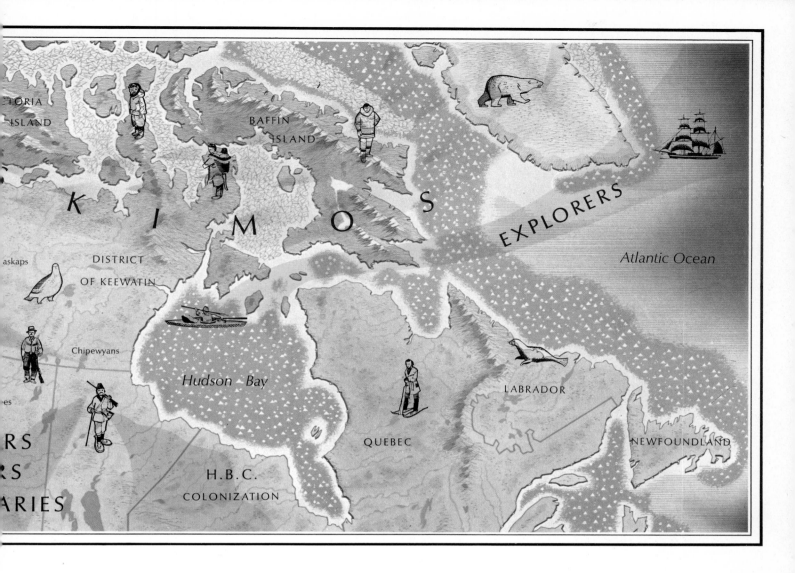

Eight thousand years ago caribou were dying on the tundra with stone points embedded in their flesh. Quartz flakes, the debris of unknown weapon-makers, lie in profusion along ancient gravel beaches that now cling crazily to hillsides three hundred feet above present water levels as the entire central Arctic continues to rise, infinitely slowly, out of the sea, rebounding from the weight of the great ice sheet. Green hummocks, hollows and circles along river banks and on the sea coast show where forgotten peoples once lived, fertilizing the sterile ground with the garbage thrown out by generations of hunters' wives. On high ridges mute mounds of shattered rock resist the millennia although the human bones they once concealed have long since vanished.

Men came early to the North. Some of them apparently came from Asia, entering the American continent along the narrow defile of unglaciated tundra lying between the Alaskan Brooks Range and the polar sea. Reaching the mouth of the Mackenzie these ancient travellers found a new world waiting to be occupied and, unlike us, they did not hesitate. Although the ice sheet had hardly departed and the climate must have been harsh, they moved steadily east and south, possibly meeting other men who had crossed from Europe and who were moving towards the west. These unknown

Eskimo stone engraving: "Man and Wife".

Asians were the ancestors of the many-faceted race that survives into our time under the generic name of Athapaskan Indians. When Europeans first reached the northwestern regions in the late eighteenth century, Athapaskans occupied the northern half of the Prairie Provinces and much of British Columbia, together with the whole of the wooded regions of the Yukon and the Northwest Territories. They appear to have numbered at least eighty thousand. The largest single group, the Chipewyans, controlled the country all the way west from Churchill to the Slave River. The Slaves, or Slavies, held the country around Great Slave Lake; to the north of them were the Dogribs and, northeast again, the Yellowknives or Copper Indians. Down the valley of the Mackenzie were the Hares and westward, among the mountains of the Yukon, were the Nahanni and the Loucheux.

The Athapaskans were not the only northern Indians. The Swampy Crees occupied the lands around the southwest and southeast shores of Hudson Bay and the Montagnais and Naskapi occupied the forests of the Labrador peninsula. The Athapaskans were a true people of the High North, which these Algonkian peoples were not. By dog sleds, canoes, on foot and on snowshoes they ranged the entire western taiga. The Chipewyans were fabulous travellers and thought little of walking from Churchill to the mouth of the Coppermine River via Great Slave Lake – a round trip of at least twenty-five hundred miles! Magnificently attuned to the taiga world, the Athapaskans knew the North as we shall never know it. Yet within fifty years of their first contacts with white men they had been so savagely decimated by our diseases, especially smallpox and measles, by liquor and by fire-arms that they were close to the vanishing point. In 1951 the entire Athapaskan population in the North numbered fewer than thirteen thousand. About eighty-five hundred remained alive in the Northwest Territories in the centennial year of 1967. The survivors do not live on reservations, for they are a Treaty people, whom we undertook to protect forever in exchange for the right to use their lands. Most of them live in desolate islands of despair around a handful of decaying trading posts such as Fort Rae, Fort Providence, Fort Franklin and Fort Good Hope. What the reputed ferocity of the arctic world was unable to do to the Athapaskans we were able to do – all too easily.

The Athapaskans were not the only truly northern people. Indeed to most Canadians they are virtually unknown, having been overshadowed by the overblown image of another race – the Eskimos.

What and who is the reality behind this jolly, chunky fellow in the bulky fur clothing standing four-square to the wild winds of a wild white world? Is he real – the smiling, simple little chap who seems to spend half his time posing for pictures at the mouth of an igloo, and the other half carving or stitching up little Ookpiks for the tourist trade? Let Jonasee of Frobisher Bay speak for his own people:

"You made a picture of us in your minds, you whites. Now you believe the picture, and you know nothing of us. You do not even know our name. You call us Eskimo. That is an Indian word. We are *Innuit* – we are *the* people of this land!"

Indeed the Eskimo is exactly what he calls himself, *Inuk*, which is to say pre-eminently man. His race may well be the toughest, most enduring, most adaptable produced by half a million years of evolution.

As early as 2000 B.C. his ancestors had occupied the most northerly regions of the North from Alaska to the east coast of northern Greenland. Presumably these people originated in Asia, although some archaeologists suspect there was an admixture with Stone Age people from the west as well. Whatever their origins, they were unbelievably capable. Their descendants occupied the whole of the tundra regions, then spread south down the Labrador coast, along the north shore of the Gulf of St. Lawrence, and down the west coast of Newfoundland as far as Cabot Strait. Some may have crossed the Strait into Nova Scotia. Many of them lived by the sea and from the sea, while still others lived far inland, deep in the Ungava Peninsula and in the Keewatin and Mackenzie plains. There was no major land area north of the taiga where they could not and did not live, except for the rock-desert islands at the very top of the Arctic Archipelago where nothing more advanced than lichens can survive. In their heyday, prior to our first coming, there may have been fifty thousand of them. Fifty thousand people for whom the high northern lands were home.

The world they lived in taught them how to make a way of life by adapting to nature rather than by trying to overmaster her. They developed a philosophy of existence that is at least as rational as most of our religions. They learned that society is at its best when human beings co-operate lovingly instead of competing fiercely. It is true they never learned to build high-rise apartments, could not fly (except in the imagination), could not have invented television, and were content to jog along (sometimes at fifteen miles an hour) behind a dog team. But then neither did they invent napalm bombs, devise poison gas, manufacture T.N.T. or nuclear weapons. Nor did they learn how to pollute, scarify, exploit and despoil the natural environment in which they lived. In the sense in which we use the word the Eskimos were not progressive; nor, if we make literacy the basic standard, were they civilized. They had no written language, but they had a very adequate alternative in a spoken language that experts consider one of the most expressive and subtle known – an evaluation that might also be applied to their carvings and prints.

Eskimos understood the true art of living. They did not simply exist. Men, women and children took a tremendous and vital joy from the hour-by-hour activities of their lives. They exercised an almost unparalleled genius at inventing and constructing *useful* equipment without benefit of engineering science or mechanical technology. There was only one thing the Eskimo lacked – he had never learned to be aggressive or acquisitive. He was far too anxious to please, to be liked, to be accommodating – and this was his undoing. Traders and whalers used his talents to enrich themselves. Missionaries savaged his philosophy in order to substitute their own. Europeans in general treated him as an inferior type of animal at the same time that they were freely begetting bastard children on his women. The delicate balance of man and nature which the Eskimos had instinctively adopted was destroyed, and the Eskimo went down to ruin. By 1950 (according to dubious, though official, census figures) there seems to have been only about three or four thousand left alive in the whole of the Canadian North; although since then they appear to have staged a remarkable comeback and, by 1966, numbered at least 11,500.

Considering the ferocious character we ascribe to the North it seems odd that this was the first region of our continent to be visited by Europeans. The first of these arrived in A.D. 982 when an Icelander named Erik the Red skippered a ship across Davis Strait to reach and explore part of the east Baffin Island coast. Being a northerner born and bred Erik recognized a good country when he saw it. Sea mammals abounded, as did sea birds; and on the land there were caribou and other highly edible mammals.

Henry Hudson lived in the world's eye only four short years. He came out of obscurity in 1607, and vanished in 1611. But in that time he made four fantastic northern voyages. In 1608 he tried to sail the rotten and leaky 40-ton Hopewell straight across the polar sea to Cathay, and he actually forced her into the polar pack to a point only 600 miles from the pole itself. The next year he tried again, this time attempting to sail northwest around the top of Europe and Asia. He got to Novaya Zemlya in the Kara Sea before the ice blocked him. Unable to find backers in England for a third voyage, he turned to the Dutch who gave him a tiny little vessel called the Half Moon, crewed by a handful of dockyard scum. Again Hudson sailed northeast, reached Novaya Zemlya — and was stopped. Instead of going home, and despite a mutinous crew, he turned west, sailed to Newfoundland, then coasted south, discovering the Hudson River. That should have been enough. Not so. In 1610 he sailed northwest again in Discovery. This time he entered Hudson Bay and reached James Bay where his crew mutinied and cast him and his son, with seven other men, adrift. Hudson and his fellows were never heard of again, although it seems likely that they landed somewhere in James Bay and that some of them survived there for a span of years.

Samuel Hearne was the Marco Polo of the Canadian Barren Lands, one of the world's great adventurers. Between 1769 and 1772 (he was only 24 when he set out), Hearne explored more than a quarter-million square miles of the northern prairie. He was the first European to see the mighty sweep of arctic coast stretching westward from the Canadian Sea to the Siberian Sea. With no other company than reluctant, and often hostile, Indians, he walked close to 5,000 miles through one of the most inaccessible territories in the world. It was so inaccessible that the last of his major areas of discovery was not revisited by white men until the 1920s.

The Icelanders who colonized Greenland made the most of Erik's western discovery and for at least two hundred years regularly visited Baffin Island on summer hunting expeditions. During those two centuries they explored south to Newfoundland where the famous "Vinland" was located, and north as far as Ellesmere Island. And they not only explored but also actually had settlements along the west coast of Ungava Bay.

Like the Eskimos the early Scandinavians were interested in the North for its own sake. But at the beginning of the sixteenth century other Europeans began to look northward for a different reason. Cut off by Spain and Portugal from voyaging to the Indies around Cape Horn and Cape of Good Hope, they dreamed of finding a usable north-west sea passage around the top of America. As early as 1508 Sebastian Cabot sailed to the northwest on behalf of England searching for a strait leading to Asia. He claimed to have got as high as 67 degrees north latitude on the Baffin Island coast and he reported the existence of a westward-trending strait (Hudson Strait), but nobody did much about it until 1576. Then the buccaneering Martin Frobisher, who was to become one of the Armada men, took up the search and explored part of Frobisher Bay. Frobisher initiated a gold rush to the northwest. In three voyages between 1585 and 1587 John Davis examined most of the coast of Davis Strait. After 1600 a determined push to find a northwest passage via Hudson Strait was begun by George Weymouth. He was followed in 1610 by Henry Hudson and later by a score of others who sailed their crank little vessels into Hudson Bay. Not until two and a half centuries later did all hope of finding a usable passage to the west die out. Meanwhile the first explorers had been followed by a different breed: the fur traders.

The Hudson's Bay Company arrived in "their" bay in 1668 and two years later received their famous charter from Charles II giving them title to all lands draining into Hudson Bay: a private kingdom that turned out to have an area of 1,422,000 square miles! The company was not unchallenged. The French gave it a good fight and at one time between 1697 and 1714 captured all but one of the company's posts. But the H.B.C. (Here Before Christ, as it is sometimes called) eventually spread across the whole of the Canadian North.

During the early nineteenth century the British made a new attempt at discovering the Northwest Passage, this time through the complex of channels of the Arctic Archipelago. The quest rose to a crescendo of activity in 1845 when Sir John Franklin with two ships and 134 men sailed west to conquer the Arctic once and for all. The result was tragedy and mystery. The entire expedition perished and to this day the story of what happened is not fully known. But the immediate result was a wave of rescue expeditions sent among the islands from the west and from the east, as well as overland along the Arctic coast. The search for Franklin's expedition resulted in the exploration of a large portion of the then unknown western and northern regions of the continent.

By 1860 the search for Franklin and for a feasible commercial passage west had both been abandoned. Explorers now turned to a more ephemeral goal—the attempt to reach the North Pole itself. What followed was a weird mélange of quixotic courage, gross stupidity, hideous suffering and international chicanery. The Pole may or may not have been reached – it hardly matters. What mattered was that this pointless quest led to the discovery of the last important land masses in North America, including many of the islands of the Queen Elizabeth group (the last of which.

Meighen Island, was not discovered until Vilhjalmur Stefansson reached it in 1916).

The exploration of the interior of the mainland had meanwhile been progressing very slowly, although it got off to a good start between 1769 and 1772 when a young Hudson's Bay man named Samuel Hearne accompanied a group of Chipewyans right across the tundra from Churchill to the Arctic coast near the mouth of the Coppermine River. After that there was little action in the interior until 1789, when the rival North West Company sent Alexander Mackenzie west and north to trace the river which bears his name. Trade followed Mackenzie and soon the western taiga filled up with fur traders, but it was three decades before the central tundra saw white men again. And as late as 1945 most of it remained unmapped.

Trading companies, independent traders, and trappers were not the only hungry men to follow the explorers into virgin territory. Close behind them came the missionaries, as avid for souls as the traders were for fur. Whalers slaughtered the Greenland whale in Baffin Bay, Hudson Strait and Hudson Bay, then turned their attention to the western arctic seas and almost exterminated the great mammals there. Gold strikes in the Yukon sent tens of thousands of white men pouring north and west to grab what they could get. As the twentieth century began, the North was one great grab-bag and the vast majority of the white men who were roaming through it were high-grading something – gold, furs, whales or souls. It was an almost totally lawless land (except for the Yukon, which was a special case) and there was no effective attempt to prevent the exploitation of natural resources or the native peoples. Nobody in the North in those days was concerned by the fact that it was Canadian territory. Prior to 1905 there was, quite literally, no government or law in what are now the Northwest Territories and Ungava, despite the fact that this had been Canadian soil for a quarter of a century and more.

Canada acquired the North by two massive grants. The first came in 1870 when the Hudson's Bay Company was persuaded by the British government to sell its private fiefdom to the new nation. At that date this commercial kingdom consisted of Rupert's Land (all the territories draining into Hudson Bay) and the Indian Territory, which included all the remaining British territory west of Hudson Bay, except British Columbia.

Canada's second acquisition, an unwanted gift if ever there was one, was the transfer to her from Britain in 1880 of all British rights to the arctic islands. This meant in effect most of the Arctic Archipelago. Thus by 1881 Canada embraced almost the limits she does today. But the nation seemed more embarrassed than pleased by the acquisition of these vast new territories. It was touch and go whether she would even bother to uphold her claims. In 1898 the great Klondike rush into the Yukon triggered a move by the United States to annex that rich territory. There were those in Ottawa even that far back who felt that any attempt to withstand the Americans would be "bad business" and might endanger commercial relations with the United States.

Fortunately not all Canadians were quite so spineless, and so a small detachment of the North West Mounted Police was sent to the Yukon to display the Canadian flag: a job they did superbly well, with the prime result that the Yukon remains a part of Canada.

In 1909 the American Robert Peary, on behalf of the U.S.A., laid claim to the North Pole and "all adjacent regions", which included most of the high arctic islands on the east – a claim that one of his associates, Donald B.

Alexander Mackenzie was 26 years of age when he set out in 1789 from Great Slave Lake on the canoe voyage he hoped would lead him to the far Pacific. A true island Scot, dour, taciturn, practical and dogged, Mackenzie sought not fame and glory, but to find a new route to wealth for the Montreal-based North-West Company, in which he was a partner. He was bitterly disappointed when the Great River which now bears his name finally led him to the Arctic Ocean. In 1793 he tried again and this time reached his goal — the Pacific coast — becoming the first European to span the continent by land. He never knew that his first discovery was by far the most important and that his Great River was destined to be one of the major avenues down which Canada would one day move into the North.

"Commander Cheyne's Proposed Method of Reaching the North Pole" —1882

The *Canadian Illustrated News* faithfully reported the Commander's fanciful plans. Balloons were in great vogue at the time and one Swedish expedition, led by Salomon Andree, did set out in 1897. Their frozen bodies were not found until 1930. Roald Amundsen's airship *Norge* did fly over the North Pole (from Spitsbergen to Alaska) in 1926 but an attempt by the Italian Nobile two years later in a similar dirigible met with disaster.

MacMillan, was still upholding as late as 1924. From 1898 to 1902 a Norwegian, Otto Sverdrup, explored much of western Ellesmere and most of Axel Heiberg, Isachsen and the Ringnes islands and laid claim to them on behalf of his own country. By the late 1800's American whalers and traders had taken *de facto* control of the western Arctic coast from Alaska to Victoria Island; of the northwestern reaches of Hudson Bay, and of much of the Baffin Island coast as well. To all of this Canada paid little heed. She did not really exert herself to claim what she had been given until the first decade of the twentieth century when a few police posts were established in Hudson Bay and one at Herschel Island west of the mouth of the Mackenzie. In 1903-4 a token Canadian arctic expedition in a Newfoundland sealing vessel, the *Neptune*, was sent north under the command of A. P. Low to proclaim Canada's official ownership of Hudson Bay and Ellesmere Island, and in the following years further voyages were made among the arctic islands to raise the flag.

These somewhat nebulous claims were not reinforced until the 1920's when Denmark showed an interest in Ellesmere Island and Canada belatedly hurried to plant detachments of the R.C.M.P. on some of the northern islands so that she could claim "effective occupation". Fortunately for us none of the other interested nations seriously attempted to dispute our claims.

Originally the whole region north and west of Upper Canada (Ontario in embryo) as far as British Columbia had been christened the Northwest Territories and divided into various districts. In 1905 the present provinces of Alberta and Saskatchewan were created. In 1912 Manitoba, Ontario and Quebec had their northern boundaries extended to their present limits. By 1912 the Northwest Territories consisted of unwanted leftovers – the districts of Mackenzie and Keewatin (sharing the balance of the remaining northern mainland between them) and the District of Franklin which encompassed the arctic islands. Except for the Yukon, which had a quasi-independence, the Northwest Territories were ruled by the Deputy Minister of the Department of the Interior (later Mines and Resources) and a council, supported by a corporal's guard of a dozen clerks and minor officials. Representatives of the two major missions, Roman Catholic and Anglican, and of the Hudson's Bay Company together with the Commissioner of the R.C.M.P. formed the appointed "council". Under this purely colonial administration of interested parties the dissolution of the Indians and Eskimos and the general spoliation of the animal resources of the North were allowed to proceed with no more than token attention from the Government of Canada.

By 1950 Indians and Eskimos alike were riddled with tuberculosis, swept by periodic epidemics of diphtheria, influenza and measles, were chronically starving and were in danger of disappearing forever from the world that had been theirs for countless centuries. Canada's record up to this date is as bad as that of any of the old colonial nations.

Paradoxically, what saved the native people by finally forcing a reluctant Canada to look northward was the impact of war which was to see the construction of the North East and North West staging routes, the Canol pipeline and the Alaska Highway. Then, much happened in a short space of time. Airfields appeared as if by magic. Weather stations were built on the outer rim of the arctic islands. Most important of all, construction started on the huge radar surveillance networks known as the Distant Early Warning Line and the Mid-Canada Early Warning Line, billion-dollar projects that brought thousands of white men temporarily into the North on construction jobs, and that finally forced the Canadian government to make

Sir John Franklin set out in 1845 in command of the best-found expedition ever sent to arctic waters to find the Northwest Passage. He had previously led two overland expeditions to the arctic coast by way of Great Slave and Great Bear Lakes. Franklin had two powerful ships and 129 picked officers and men. After speaking to some whalers off Greenland in July 1845, men and ships vanished. To this day, nobody knows the details of what happened. Apparently the ships were caught in the ice off the coast of Prince of Wales Island, and were eventually abandoned. Franklin died and was buried, and his men then set out to walk south to safety. None of them made it. The greatest search in arctic history began with more than 40 expeditions eventually in the field. The bones of some of Franklin's men were found on Prince of Wales Island by Leopold McClintock in 1858. In 1923 the Danish explorer, Knud Rasmussen, found the greening bones of a large party on the mainland coast near the mouth of the Back River. In 1931 another group of skeletons was discovered on the Todd Islands. Fewer than two-thirds of the men who left their ships have so far been accounted for.

Vilhjalmur Stefansson, a Canadian of Icelandic parentage, was the most active, successful and many-faceted explorer of the Canadian Arctic in modern times. All his life he fought apathy and opposition to his efforts to persuade Canada to look northward. Because he was unyielding in his belief that Canada's future lay in the North, he was hated by many people in power. He died in the U.S. in 1962. In his biggest expedition, he remained north of the Arctic Circle for five years, 1913-18. In 1952, Stefansson Island in the central Arctic was named after him.

some attempt at effective administration of its northern colony. It had taken just eighty years for Canada to "discover" the North and make the first tentative move toward accepting it as part of the nation.

Today the missions, traders and R.C.M.P. no longer rule the North. More and more government departments are taking part in its development and administration. The Department of Transport operates ships, communication systems, weather stations and airports; the Department of Indian Affairs and Northern Development looks to the needs of the natives and to the exploration and development of natural resources; the Northern Health Service provides nursing and hospitalization; the military occupy many posts; the Department of Fisheries oversees fishing and sea mammals. The North has come a long way toward joining the rest of the nation since 1950, but it still has a long, long way to go before the effects of the years of apathy and ignorance will be overcome.

Even now the battle to emancipate the North is by no means won. Powerful voices still maintain that Indians and Eskimos are simple, primitive peoples who cannot be expected to cope with the complexities of our modern world and who should remain isolated under a form of benevolent paternalism – which can be equated with continued colonialism. This fallacious concept is based on the assumption that Eskimos and Indians today are what they were a hundred years ago. Nothing could be further from the truth. One of the "open" secrets of the white individuals and organizations that have for so long ruled the North is the fact that there probably is not now, and has not been for a long time, any such thing as a racially discrete Eskimo or Indian. Traders, trappers, missionaries, policemen, explorers, whalers, have all done their vigorous best to "improve the breed". To what extent they have succeeded is a moot question, but there is no doubt that they have left their mark. The northern blood is now a mixture of European, Eskimo and Indian with slight admixtures of other types, including Negro. If it were not for our racist insistence on maintaining arbitrary distinctions between white, Indian, Métis and Eskimo, I suspect the northerners might have become one people in practice, as they are becoming in biological reality. And that, I submit, would have been a very good thing for all concerned as well as for this country we call Canada.

Rear-Admiral Sir John Ross, searching for the Northwest Passage in 1818, meets his first Eskimos.

PEOPLE OF THE NORTH

There are many great races of men in the world, some numbering in the multi-millions. Eskimos belong to a people who number under 70,000, of whom nearly 13,000 are Canadians. They are a 'small people' but they are superlative individual human beings. Quality is their strength—not quantity. Superficially, they may seem different from us; even repulsive in terms of the external trappings of two vastly dissimilar cultures. Yet, in true essentials, this man is just ourself not yet alienated from the reality of natural existence in a natural world.

This is Zachary Itteemangnak, of Pelly Bay, N.W.T. He takes his fish as fresh as he can get it.

INDIAN skills were an intelligent response to necessity. Imagination, resourcefulness, the materials at hand – these were the primary keys to living for men like these Naskapi canoe-builders at Northwest River, in the thin spruce and larch forests of Labrador.

The Natives

The Eskimos and northern Indians are two 'small peoples' sharing a vast world. Like the Eskimos, the taiga Indians have suffered terrible attrition from contact with us. They have endured chronic starvation, endemic disease and monumental neglect – and have somehow survived! True peoples of adversity, they have a silent strength, an unshakeable steadfastness and indomitable will. They are an integral part of the northern world for it is *their* world. We have much to offer them, and they are standing ready at the door – not as beggars, but rich in their unique ability, rich in comprehension, rich in enduring strength. For good or evil, they want to make one cause with us . . . if we will let them.

Children accept chores early in the makeshift homes but there's no discipline: Indian children do as they please. They will be lucky to get 90 days schooling every year.

This Dogrib woman shared a tent with seven other Indians at Fort Rae, N.W.T.

ESKIMO mother Kidlak bathes her youngest child Ruthee while her three sons romp. This is the family of Idlouk, an outstanding Baffin Island Eskimo living in a wood-and-sod house near Pond Inlet. The time was mid-February and the house was buried by snow; inside temperature was 75 deg., with heat from three seal-oil lamps. Most Eskimos never take a bath in their lives.

Once a great bear hunter, elderly Akomalik stays home to scrape white fox skins. Pages from picture magazines insulate the hut walls and reflect light.

Fred Carpenter, son of a white whaler, was once the richest Eskimo; now his big boat is for sale.

The Whites

Until recently, whites in the North were few and far between and their control of the country was wildly out of proportion to their numbers. Explorers came and went leaving little imprint except in terms of bastard offspring; they were closely followed by more tenacious aliens. First came the traders who, through two centuries, formed the core of the northern aristocracy and governed the land like liege lords. They were soon followed by the missionaries who undertook to "civilize" the natives and arrange their eventual entry into heaven. White trappers and prospectors began to drift north, but were looked on askance; it was partly to keep them in their places that pseudo-government in the shape of the Mounted Police arrived on the scene. The police, too, were aristocrats and set up the third of the three ruling classes of the North. These usually charitable autocrats exercised what was called a "benevolent paternal influence on the unlettered and child-like savages" . . . whose land, in fact, this was.

TRADER
Frank Fisher, at Lake Harbour in 1918, was a typical servant of the then-omnipotent Hudson's Bay Co.

MISSIONARY
The wife of famed Bishop Bompas was posed, with props, in the Montreal studio of the pioneer photographer, William Notman.

POLICEMAN
Bearded Corporal Dempster, North West Mounted Police, pictured after his great feat in finding the lost Fitzgerald patrol in 1911.

PROSPECTOR
Albert Faille grew old searching Headless Valley, N.W.T., for his own Eldorado. This photo was taken on the Nahanni in 1961.

THE JUDGE

By the 1950's more white men of a new stripe were beginning to concern themselves with conditions in the North. Foremost among them was Judge John Howard Sissons who set out to bring justice to the natives. Here he questions a witness on a theft case. Sissons brought a new concept to the North — the idea that an Indian or an Eskimo was the white man's equal.

THE PRIEST

Father van der Velde, an Oblate priest, spent much of his life in the remote Eskimo settlement of Pelly Bay. He was convinced the natives should be segregated, and protected from the outer world. Most of the men of this remarkable order – there are about sixty of them in the North – come from France direct to posts in the Arctic. They get home leave only once a decade.

Who raised this cairn? Did a lost colony of Vikings once inhabit Ungava? This rocky tower, 10 feet high, stands like a guidepost on the Payne River, leading to an ancient inland townsite. The strange ruins were not discovered until 1967.

The Unknown Forerunners From the Western World

Most of us blindly believe the history books but forget that historians only record events about which they have indisputable proof. Thus history tells us Columbus discovered America and the first European to see Canada's North was probably Sebastian Cabot in 1509. Nevertheless, there are Scandinavian sagas surviving from the 12th century which tell of routine voyages to the Canadian North, and of quasi-permanent settlements, between about 1000 and 1400 A.D. Scholars mostly wrote off these accounts as pure invention;

Bearing the appearance of the Norse legendary Hammer of Thor, this weird construction puzzles archeologists. Some scholars doubt its age but research on Scandinavian sagas indicates immigrants reached present-day Quebec in 1100.

Standing thirty miles up the coast from the mouth of Payne River, this 10 ft. cairn is one of a chain (each visible from the other) that probably guided early voyagers. Only superior sailors could negotiate the 45-foot tides of Payne Bay.

now they are not so sure. It begins to look as if European voyagers from Greenland, sailing seven or eight centuries ago, were nearly as familiar with east Baffin Island and Davis Strait as we are today. It also looks as if the mysterious disappearance of an entire Scandinavian settlement from west Greenland in the early 14th century may have been the result of mass emigration to the shores of Ungava Bay. In any event, a stubborn, maverick archeologist named Thomas Lee from Laval University has uncovered scores of ancient sites in the

Ungava region which bear little similarity to old Eskimoan ruins, but which *do* bear a startling resemblance to contemporary Scandinavian, and even Celtic, sites in Greenland, Iceland, north Ireland and the Scottish islands. Reports of Lee's work have been scoffed at by arm-chair authorities, but those who (like the author) have seen them are not so much surprised by Lee's hypothesis as they are by the restraint and caution with which he evaluates what may well be the greatest archeological discovery yet in the Canadian North.

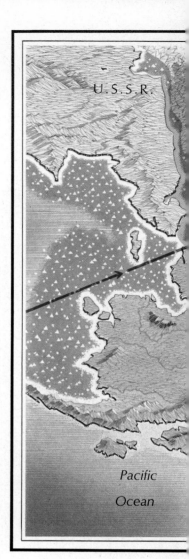

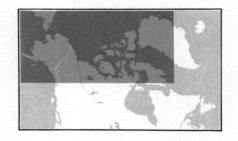

3

The Floating Lands

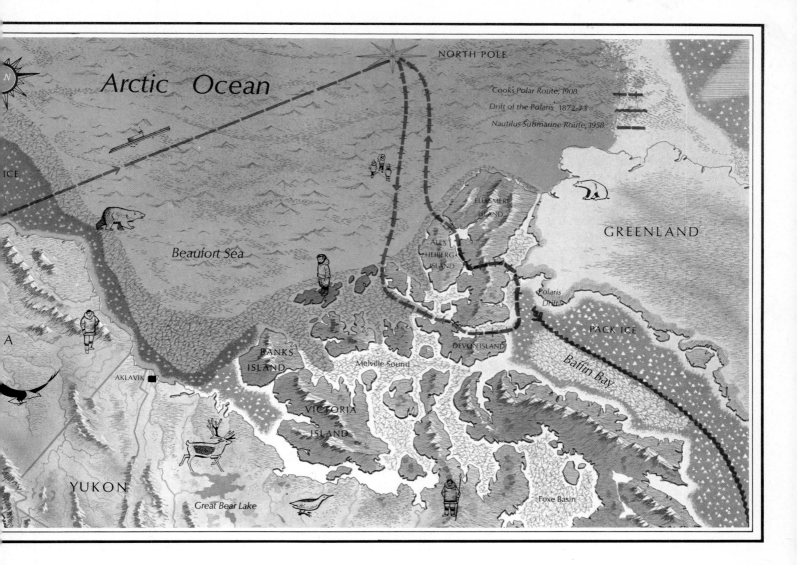

Arctic Ocean

NORTH POLE

ICE

Beaufort Sea

ELLESMERE ISLAND

GREENLAND

ALEX HEIBERG ISLAND

Polaris Drift

A

PACK ICE

BANKS ISLAND

Melville Sound

DEVON ISLAND

Baffin Bay

AKLAVIK

VICTORIA ISLAND

YUKON

Great Bear Lake

Foxe Basin

When ancient geographers of the Greek world conceived of a polar continent lying far to the north of all known lands they were not so terribly wrong, even though what they had in mind was a land of rock and soil. The Arctic Ocean, of which Canada claims to own a formidable chunk, *is* land in essence, and one of considerable variety.

Basically this floating continent, in its mediterranean basin embraced by Asia, Europe, Greenland and North America, consists of heavy ice called the polar pack, and ranges from five to fifteen feet in thickness. Great sheets of the pack ice crowd against and upon one another to form ranges of hills called pressure ridges. Or they separate, forming intricate patterns of open rivers and streams called leads. In some areas there are large open "lakes" of salt water – polynias – that do not freeze and disappear. In summer fresh-water ponds and even streams appear on the surface of the pack, for although new sea ice is salty, the salt gradually seeps out and water melting from the old sea ice is quite fresh.

Of real mountains there are none, but they are approximated by icebergs which can be several hundred feet high and as much as two miles long. They

The dreaded icebergs of the ancient mariners often reach Nova Scotian shores and some drift to the Azores.

are found in such numbers in north Baffin Bay that whalers and explorers sometimes mistook them for distant mountain ranges.

As early as 1910 explorers were reporting what they believed to be land islands far out in the polar pack. Real islands actually do exist, but they are composed of ice, not rock. They are among the strangest features of the floating lands. Some are only a few miles square, but at least one has been reported twenty miles long by fifteen wide and nearly two hundred feet thick. The ice of these islands is extremely ancient – more than three thousand years old, according to carbon 14 tests. Their coasts rise thirty to forty feet above the surrounding pack and their surfaces are rolling plateaus dotted, in summer, with fresh-water ponds and streamlets. They are probably break-aways from a vast shelf of land-fast solid ice, hundreds of feet thick, which projects out into the polar basin from the northern shores of Ellesmere Island and north Greenland. Since they were first discovered (from the air in 1947) more than a dozen have been kept under observation and occasionally occupied as scientific stations.

In many parts of our North the continental land grades into the floating land so imperceptibly that a man can walk off the coast and never know he is over the hidden sea. When flying over the archipelago in winter it is often impossible to tell whether you are over ice or land. The most northern islands – Ellesmere, Axel Heiberg, Meighen, the Ringnes group, Borden and Mackenize King – are perpetually welded together by pack ice, so that ice and rock together form one single land larger than Newfoundland.

Parts of the floating land, such as those lying close to the coasts, are static; but the floating polar continent itself is anything but. Slowly this whole great world of ice revolves around its basin taking as much as five years to make a circuit. The patterns shift from day to day. While the currents steadily propel the entire mass, surface winds send portions of it on conflicting courses so that leads open and close and the clash of great pans in collision raises new pressure ridges. Living on the polar pack can be a bit like living in an earthquake zone.

The size of the floating lands is not constant. In "good ice years" the frozen continent shrinks in upon itself and ships can ply far to the north. During "bad ice years" it enlarges until it blocks the approaches to the Arctic Ocean as well as most of the channels among the arctic islands. Each year the polar pack loses about one-fifth of its area in the form of drift ice that floats south out of the polar basin on two frigid oceanic rivers – the East Greenland and the Labrador currents. The pack that comes down through Baffin Bay and along the Labrador coast on the Canadian front is often nearly as solid as the polar pack itself – it forms a gigantic ice tongue, mottled with icebergs, thrusting down into the Atlantic as far as Nova Scotia. Individual icebergs from it have even drifted as far south as the Azores. But what the floating polar continent loses in this way it regenerates each winter in the form of newly frozen ice.

Oddly enough, the climate of the floating continent is more moderate than that of the nearby solid lands. At the North Pole the temperature seldom reaches thirty degrees below zero and during the six months of perpetual daylight – the long arctic summer – it sometimes rises to fifty degrees above.

Like all lands the floating world has its own life forms. There are no true plants on the ice, but there is an abundance of animal life. Vilhjalmur Stefansson once spent ninety-six days and walked five hundred miles across the polar pack of the Beaufort Sea, during which time he and his men lived almost exclusively on seals shot in open leads. The Eskimos have always known about the animal riches of the ice world and they spear seals at breathing holes in the pack or shoot them in the leads. Walrus are killed along the fringes of the pack. Narwhals (the sea-unicorn of ancient times) are found in leads far from the nearest open water. Polar bears roam freely over the ice and arctic foxes follow after, scavenging the leavings of the ice king. The largest herds of seals existing in the world today congregate in spring on the ice driving south to Labrador and Newfoundland where they bear their young in untold thousands.

All of these animals take their livelihood directly or indirectly from the hidden sea below the ice. The polar basin is tremendously deep – some parts of it reaching a depth of nearly three miles – and relatively sterile. But the surface layers near its fringes are enormously rich in minute forms of plant and animal life known as plankton. These feed the fishes and also feed (or used to) vast numbers of the great baleen whales that once populated Baffin Bay and the northern coastal waters until they were almost exterminated by the whaling fleets.

That man too can live and travel on the floating land has long been known. In 1827 a British naval officer, Edward Parry, led a party of seamen on a walk to the Pole from Spitsbergen; but the ice drifted south under his feet almost as fast as he could trek to the north. Other attempts were made from the Spitsbergen area but it was from the coast of Ellesmere Island that the longest polar walks were made, culminating in 1908 and 1909 in the possible attainment of the Pole itself by two Americans, Cook and Peary. Of the two, Cook's was the more remarkable journey. Travelling with only two Eskimo companions he lived on the floating lands from March 14, 1908, until he regained solid land on July 4, 1909. After these two came Stefansson, born a Canadian of Icelandic parents, he became a naturalized American and then, in 1913, he became Canadian again. Between 1913 and 1918 Stefansson lived and travelled all through the High Arctic Archipelago and far out over the polar sea as well.

These were intentional travels; there have also been some unintentional ones of note. On October 15, 1872, the American arctic exploring ship *Polaris* was nipped in the ice at the very head of Baffin Bay and nineteen of her crew, including (fortunately for the white men) two Eskimo families, were marooned on the pack. They drifted south on it well over two thousand miles until, on April 30 of the following year, they were rescued near the shores of central Labrador by the *Tigress*, a Newfoundland sealing vessel.

During all this time they kept alive and well by eating seals and sea birds killed by the two Eskimo men in the party. There was nothing lifeless or sterile about that portion of the floating lands.

Several attempts have also been made to penetrate the ice lands by ship. The most spectacularly successful was the voyage of the Norwegian ship *Fram* commanded by Fridtjof Nansen. In 1893 Nansen allowed the specially constructed *Fram* to be frozen into the polar pack off the central Russian coast. The stout little vessel then drifted – a sort of house in the ice – for nearly three years, right across the polar basin to emerge on the other side near Spitsbergen.

The idea was a good one, but who needed a ship? In 1937 a Soviet party, led by Ivan Papanin, landed several four-engined aircraft on the ice near the North Pole and set up a scientific station on the floating lands. They remained in possession for 274 days until they were taken off by a Soviet icebreaker in the Greenland Sea after a comfortable drift of 1,300 miles.

—Illustration of narwhal by 16th century artist who never saw one. (See modern photograph on page 90.)

"Upon a small island was found a great dead fish which, so it seemed, had been embalmed with ice. It was round like to a porpoise, being about twelve foot long, and having a horn of two yards length growing out of the snout or nostrils. This horn is wreathed and straight, like in fashion to a taper made of wax, and may truly be thought to be the sea Unicorn. This horn is to be reserved as a jewel by the Queen Majesties commandment, in her wardrobe of robes."
– Description from The Three Voyages of Martin Frobisher, *1578.*

Rear-Admiral Sir William Edward Parry joined the Royal Navy at 13 and, by age 35, had made three unsuccessful attempts to find the Northwest Passage. He did find and name Hecla and Fury Strait – a true entrance to the Passage – Barrow Strait and, of course, the Parry Islands.

"It was marvellous in a region apparently so unfavourable to reproduction, what a perfect warren of rats we had on board. Their impudence increased with their numbers. They harboured amongst the men's bedding and showed such boldness in fight and such dexterity in dodging missiles that they were tolerated as an inevitable nuisance. They are everywhere, under the stove, in the steward's locker, in our cushions, in our beds. If I was asked what, after darkness and cold and scurvy are the three besetting curses of our Arctic sojourn, I should say, rats, rats, rats. A mother rat bit my finger to the bone last Friday as I was intruding my hand into a bearskin mitten she had chosen for a homestead. I withdrew my hand with instinctive courtesy but amongst them the rats carried off the mitten before I could suck the finger."

– Dr. Elisha Kane, 1856.

Air exploration of the floating continent began early. In 1897 a young Swede, Salomon Andrée, and two companions set out from Spitsbergen to drift across the Pole in a free balloon; the expedition vanished until the bodies of the three men were found frozen in an ice bank on White Island, east of Spitsbergen, in 1930.

From about 1914, when the Soviets made the first airplane flight over the polar ice, a steady stream of airborne explorers have flown over the ice continent. In 1926 a flight was undertaken by Roald Amundsen and Lincoln Ellsworth in the dirigible *Norge* and this unwieldy monster successfully flew from Spitsbergen to Alaska. When a sister ship, the *Italia*, commanded by Umberto Nobile, attempted a similar flight in 1928, she crashed onto the polar pack with a heavy loss of life.

The Soviets set the pace in arctic flying. During the late 1930's they sent several aircraft right across the Pole to North America. One of the early flights landed in Nova Scotia, but in 1937 another aircraft flew non-stop from the U.S.S.R. to Mexico and then turned back to land in California!

Airplane flights over the polar continent quickly became routine. The Soviets have made more than two thousand landings, and both they and the Americans are now landing multi-engined aircraft there almost at will. The floating continent has become a busy place. It is even inhabited by man on a continuing basis. The Americans have periodically occupied some of the ice islands, while the Soviets maintain many research stations on the main pack.

Interest in travel over the floating ice is by no means dead among the general public. Within the last five years two expeditions have attempted to cross the polar continent, one on skis and the other on motorcycles. In both expeditions the members were perhaps a little too optimistic, for neither succeeded.

Not all the polar explorations have been across or above the floating lands. As far back as 1931 Sir Hubert Wilkins conceived the idea of crossing the Arctic Ocean beneath the ice and he talked the U.S. Navy into selling him for $1 an outmoded submarine which he re-christened *Nautilus*. This particular *Nautilus* was not up to the job. It remained for another *Nautilus*, nuclear powered, to reach the Pole from the underside in 1958. Since then both Soviet and U.S. nuclear submarines have cruised most of the polar basin and under-ice voyages have become commonplace.

Surface ships have been active too. In the 1950's the Royal Canadian Navy commissioned a fine new icebreaker, H.M.C.S. *Labrador*, and in 1955 *Labrador* made the first northwest passage from the Atlantic to the Pacific by a deep-draft ship (the passage had previously been made only by small wooden vessels).

The need to supply the DEW Line sites led to a rapid increase in Canada's fleet of icebreakers as this country (reversing the usual trend) took over a going concern from the United States. Consequently in this one area Canada has really moved north. The Canadian Coast Guard Service of the Department of Transport now operates a fleet of ice-going ships second only to that of the Soviets. In 1965 sixteen Canadian Coast Guard vessels plus five others chartered by the Department carried one hundred thousand tons of freight to northern outposts. In 1967 the C.G.S. fleet numbered ten full icebreakers, including the *Labrador*, taken over from the Navy. One of the new ones is the most powerful conventionally powered icebreaker in the world (24,000 h.p.), second only to the nuclear-powered *Lenin* (44,000 h.p.) belonging to the U.S.S.R. For Canadian seamen – most of them from Newfoundland, Nova

Scotia and Quebec – the North holds no special terrors. For them it is a place where men live and do their work – and they are doing their work supremely well.

The Soviets long ago recognized the potential value of the arctic mediterranean sea and they now have by far the biggest icebreaking fleet in the world. *Lenin*, the pride of their fleet, has proved that ice navigation is possible even deep within the fringes of the ice continent, and she would be capable of opening surface routes across portions of the Arctic Ocean to North America. The U.S.S.R.'s Northern Sea Route runs six thousand miles along the Arctic coast from Murmansk in Europe to the Bering Sea on the Pacific. Ships make the direct run in three weeks, and more than two million tons of cargo goes "across the top" each year. Even foreign ships are now using the Northern Sea Route as a short-cut between European and Pacific coasts. Unhappily the full potential of the arctic mediterranean sea remains frozen – not by the climate but by the cold war. If this unnatural animosity between northern neighbours could be eased, the polar world could come into its own. Trans-polar flights – at present undertaken only in a minor way – provide by far the shortest routes between North America and many parts of Asia and Europe. In 1966 the U.S.S.R. began a direct arctic air service between Moscow and Montreal. The feasibility of transpolar shipping using heavy icebreakers, reinforced merchant vessels and nuclear-powered merchant submarines has been established beyond question. Even low-value bulk cargoes, such as oil from the Canadian North, could be moved economically across the northern mediterranean sea by employing submerged barges, perhaps made of plastic, towed by nuclear submarine tugs. The time may come when the political climate will thaw sufficiently to allow a rational use of the Arctic Ocean as a bridge between three continents. If and when this happens, Canada will be in an extraordinarily advantageous position – always assuming she has not by then lost effective control of her arctic seas to a more ambitious or more far-seeing nation.

Canada can be proud of its present ice-breaking fleet: ten full icebreakers, ranging from the old Saurel *(3,000 H.P.- built in 1929) to the* John A. Macdonald *(15,000 H.P. - 1960). Two new ships will soon join the fleet and one of them will be the most powerful non-nuclear icebreaker in the world. With 24,000 horsepower, driven by triple screws, she will be a match for most of the ice conditions that might be encountered in the Canadian Arctic.*

A chance meeting in Hudson Strait, July 16, 1821: Hecla *and* Fury *of the second Parry expedition meet a load of Swiss settlers in the* Lord Wellington, *bound for the Red River Colony, and the two H.B.C. vessels,* Prince of Wales *and* Eddystone.

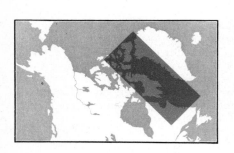

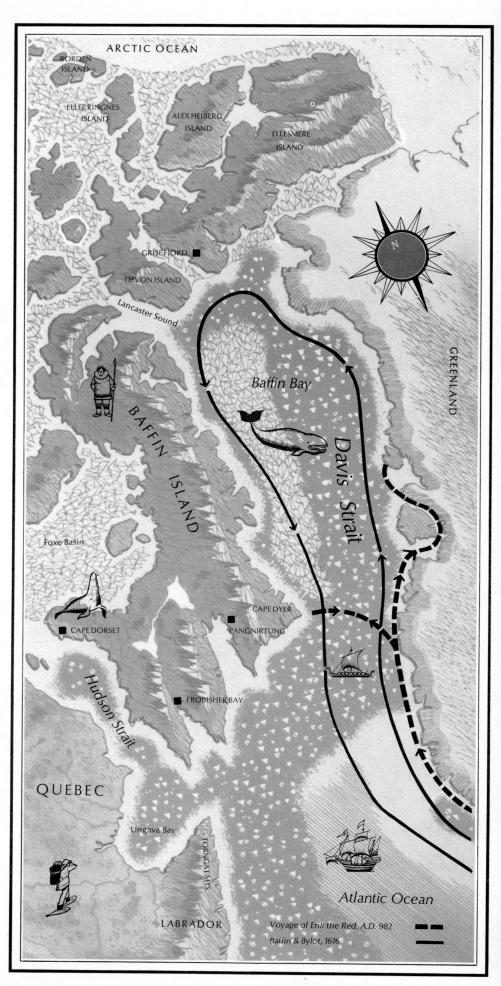

ARCTIC OCEAN

BORDEN
ISLAND

ELLEF RINGNES
ISLAND

ALEX HEIBERG
ISLAND

ELLESMERE
ISLAND

N

GRISE FIORD

DEVON ISLAND

Lancaster Sound

Baffin Bay

GREENLAND

Davis Strait

BAFFIN ISLAND

Foxe Basin

CAPE DYER

CAPE DORSET

PANGNIRTUNG

FROBISHER BAY

Hudson Strait

QUEBEC

Ungava Bay

TORNGAT MTS.

Atlantic Ocean

LABRADOR

Voyage of Erik the Red, A.D. 982

Baffin & Bylot, 1616

The Icy Mountains

4

Curving up the east coast of northern Canada like a gigantic sickle runs one of the world's great mountain ranges. Although it is nineteen hundred miles long, few Canadians are aware that it exists. The range as a whole does not even have a name.

The southern half of the sickle's handle forms the mountain peninsula of northern Labrador, the ominously named Torngat Mountains (*torngat* is Eskimo for sorcerer). Bleak, barren, snow-capped even in summer, standing with their feet in the Atlantic, some of their mighty cliffs fall three thousand feet sheer into the thundering ocean. It is a weird and desolate region shunned throughout time by man except for a few Eskimos who tried to survive in its black-walled fiords – and failed. Almost one thousand years ago Thorfin Karlsefni and Bjarni Herjolfsson, sailing to and from Greenland, were appalled by the grim face of the Torngats. They called it Helluland and described it as a "worthless country". Early Breton fishermen who fished off its shores knew it as *Terre sterile*, and it is truly one of the few parts of the North to deserve the name. Despite its southerly location it is relatively devoid of animal life, although the sea nearby is rich in marine life. Much of the interior of the Torngats remains unexplored. The region boasts no mines, has nothing to draw men to it, and its raw desolation engenders such an awesome atmosphere that the few white men who have lingered on its coasts have been inclined to accept the Eskimo belief that it is a haunted land.

Northward across Hudson Strait, on Baffin Island, lies the upper portion of the handle, composed of the Everett Mountains of Meta Incognita Peninsula and the unnamed ranges of Hall Peninsula, separated from each other by the great gash of Frobisher Bay.

The sickle's blade begins at the Cumberland Peninsula in a welter of peaks, fiords and glaciers. With heights of eight thousand feet it curves to the north along the east coast of Baffin Bay to the top of Ellesmere Island. It is an icy blade that well deserves the name Icy Mountains.

The Icy Mountains form the fiord-riven eastern coast of Baffin Island, including Bylot Island. Pierced by Lancaster Sound the mountains march north across eastern Devon Island, gaining breadth and height until they occupy almost all of Ellesmere and Axel Heiberg islands, reaching altitudes above ten thousand feet. They seem to be heading for the Pole itself and, in fact, they reach it – beneath the surface of the frozen sea. From northern Ellesmere Island they continue as a submarine range, the Lomonosov Ridge, seven thousand feet above the floor of the polar basin (which they divide

"I cannot resist saying that the word 'sport' has a curious meaning when applied to killing muskox. I have heard of long journeys being made and even of ships being outfitted for the purpose of hunting muskox. There may be much to say for the pleasures and even the adventures of the journey itself, but as for the 'hunting' I would suggest that equally good 'sport' could be secured with far less trouble and expense by paying some farmer for the permission of going into his pasture and killing his cows."

– Vilhjalmur Stefansson.

into two unequal parts) passing over the North Pole and then running south until they emerge as the New Siberian Islands on the Arctic coast of the Soviet Union. If we take into account this lengthy underwater extension, the whole range is more than three thousand miles long!

The Icy Mountains crowd down to the sea so that they loom as high above an observer as the famous peaks of the Rockies, whose bases are set several thousand feet above sea level. The fiords gouged into them by glaciers of a vanished age are among the most spectacular anywhere and one of them, Admiralty Inlet on north Baffin, is the longest in the world. But it is not their size alone that makes the Icy Mountains so impressive: it is the fact that they carry on their shoulders one of the greatest collections of glaciers outside Greenland and Antarctica. These spill down the steep slopes to the heads of the cavernous fiords, where they calve their icebergs. In the interior valleys moraines of vanished glaciers, themselves looming like miniature mountain ranges of gravel and sand, produce intricate patterns that seem totally alien to our planet. In addition to the glaciers there are the icecaps, two major ones on Baffin Island, one on Devon, and at least five on Ellesmere and Axel Heiberg islands. These are immense plateaus of solid ice, many hundreds of feet thick, through which protrude the black, broken teeth of buried mountains. The icecaps alone cover over forty thousand square miles – an area the size of Ireland. They are survivors of the ice sheet that once covered much of Canada; now they lurk in the far reaches of the North like insensate monsters, but waiting patiently for the day when they can begin creeping southward to regain the world they lost ten thousand years ago.

The country of the Icy Mountains seems lifeless at first glance, but in the deep valleys there is often lush tundra growth, and here the muskox is king, attended by wolves and foxes. About the turn of the century the muskox herds in this region were almost exterminated by whalers and by explorers heading for the Pole. They are slowly recovering from the slaughter: there may be five or six thousand on Axel Heiberg, Ellesmere and Devon islands. None now exist on Baffin Island, but caribou are found in all four islands and appear to be on the increase too. Arctic hares and ptarmigan are abundant in their cycles, and the great sea cliffs harbour colonies of birds running into the millions; while eider ducks nest on the innumerable offshore islands.

The sea that roars at the feet of the Icy Mountains is singularly rich. Seals, walrus, narwhals, white whales and true whales abound in the south-flowing Labrador Current. Sea and land together once provided a good livelihood for some of the most northerly dwelling peoples the world has ever known: the Eskimos of Smith Sound at the head of Baffin Bay. These people once lived and hunted over all of Ellesmere and Axel Heiberg. Now these vast islands, larger than Great Britain, have almost no inhabitants.

The Icy Mountains were early glimpsed by Europeans. In A.D. 982 Erik the Red saw the glittering peaks and ice fields of the Cumberland Peninsula of Baffin Island from a mountain top in Greenland and sailed across Davis Strait to investigate, thereby becoming the discoverer of a new continent. Within a few decades the crossing had become commonplace and by 1250 Norsemen from Greenland seem to have visited most of the coasts of the Icy Mountains.

The first "modern" European to see them was probably John Davis who, on his first arctic voyage in 1585, reached Cape Dyer on the Cumberland Peninsula. In 1616 Robert Bylot (already a veteran of three incredibly tough northwestern voyages), accompanied by William Baffin, made a complete circumnavigation of Baffin Bay and made a record distance north that held for 236 years. Baffin wrote the subsequent report and so got the credit for one of the great arctic voyages of all time. Bylot followed the Icy Mountains south from Ellesmere Island to Cape Dyer and Baffin plotted the mouths of Smith, Jones and Lancaster sounds. But their discoveries were so far ahead of the sluggish minds at home that Baffin was labelled a liar and for the next two centuries the very existence of the great bay that bears his name was denied by geographers. The Icy Mountains were not seen again by Europeans until 1818 when Sir John Ross repeated Bylot's voyage and demonstrated that Baffin had told nothing but the truth. During the late nineteenth century, explorers by the score sailed north under the white mountains searching through Lancaster Sound for the Northwest Passage and later through Smith Sound for the Pole. But explorers were outnumbered by whalers, mainly Scots in the early days, who hunted Baffin Bay in hundreds of ships. The fiords of the Icy Mountains were used both as whaling grounds and as wintering quarters. Nearly a century of contact between whalers and Eskimos resulted in the emergence of a new, mixed and singularly hardy people on the east shores of Baffin Island.

Farther north, between 1898 and 1902, Otto Sverdrup explored most of western Ellesmere Island and discovered Axel Heiberg, Ellef and Amund Ringnes, and Findlay islands, which he claimed for Norway. Norway hesitated long enough for Canada to send A. P. Low north in 1903 in command of the Dominion Government Expedition to Hudson Bay and the Arctic Islands in the Newfoundland sealer *Neptune*, to read a proclamation annexing the arctic islands to the Dominion. Many years later our government paid Sverdrup's estate $67,000 in "recognition of his work". It was a small price for a land that may one day be as valuable to us as Alaska (purchased from Russia) became to the United States. But we did not attempt legal occupation of the islands until 1922, when the R.C.M.P. established a post at Craig Harbour, and in 1926 another on Bache Peninsula, both on Ellesmere; in 1924, a post at Dundas Harbour on Devon Island, and in 1927 one at Lake Harbour on Ellesmere Island. These stations have since been abandoned and the only remaining detachment in the Sverdrup group is a police post at Grise Fiord on the south coast of Ellesmere, where a number of Eskimo families have also been transplanted from farther south to form Canada's most northerly settlement. There are two other tiny clusters of humanity on the islands, at the weather stations of Eureka and Alert; but they were established jointly by the U.S.A. and Canada at American suggestion and it is a moot question who really owns them.

Devon Island, south of Ellesmere Island, is totally uninhabited, but Baffin Island is relatively populous. Baffin looms large in the early history of the North, for it was on its southern portion that buccaneering Martin Frobisher, later one of Sir Francis Drake's sea-going companions, made his landfall in 1576 during a voyage in search of the Northwest Passage. Frobisher entered the bay that now bears his name (he was convinced that it was a strait leading to the west), but the discovery of what he took to be gold diverted him to a new purpose. The next year he was back in his "strait" with two ships and the following year he led a flotilla of thirteen vessels to this new King Solomon's Mine. The expedition brought with it the first prefabricated house ever to arrive in the North and unwittingly set a fashion that is still very much in vogue. When Frobisher's ore-laden flotilla returned home it was finally decided that the stuff was worthless iron pyrites. The

These small Beluga (or White) whales, weighing about 1200 lbs. and running to 12 feet in length, are sometimes called "Sea Canaries" because of the squeaky noises they make. Sociable, garrulous and friendly, they are abundant in northern seas and are now being caught commercially in Hudson Bay and on the western arctic coast. Beluga Muktuk (the jellied outer skin) is now available in cans to adventurous gourmets.

Although the arctic climate is not half as bad as most people like to think, it can be very cold. Oddly enough the coldest regions are not those farthest to the north. In Canada the lowest temperatures ever recorded were −81.4° at the town of Snag, well south in the Yukon. But Canada is lucky. Oymyakon, in east central Siberia, is the coldest place on the face of our globe and temperatures of −96° have been recorded there.
Also contrary to what most people think, the farther north you go the less snow there is. In the high arctic islands annual precipitation is less than two inches, about the same as many desert areas.

Hudson Bay lemming
– *drawn from nature by J. W. Audubon*

Lemmings à la Crème

1 dozen fat lemmings
1 cup white flour
salt and pepper
cloves
ethyl alcohol
1 piece sowbelly (or ordinary salt pork)

Skin and gut the mice but do not remove the heads, wash, then place in a pot with enough alcohol to cover the carcasses. Allow to marinate for about 2 hrs. and cut sowbelly into small cubes and fry slowly until most of the fat has been rendered. Now remove the carcasses from the alcohol and roll them in a mixture of salt, pepper and flour. Then place in frying pan and sauté for 5 minutes, being careful not to allow the pan to get too hot or the delicate meat will dry out and become tough. Now add a cup of alcohol and 6 or 8 cloves and cover pan and allow to simmer slowly for 15 minutes. The cream sauce can be made according to any standard recipe. When the sauce is ready, drench the carcasses with it, cover and allow to rest in a warm place for 10 minutes before serving.

bubble burst and the location of the mine and of Frobisher's "strait" itself was lost until 1861 when a Yankee explorer named Charles Francis Hall stumbled by accident upon the relics of Frobisher's shore base and so restored to the world the knowledge of a forgotten venture.

Frobisher would have trouble recognizing his old stamping ground today. The head of his bay is now the site of one of the largest settlements in the Canadian North – and one of the most depressing. During the last war the U.S.A. spent millions to establish an air base at the foot of the bay. A few years after the war the airfield was a major refuelling point for a number of airlines flying piston-engined aircraft on Great Circle routes to Europe. Frobisher Bay grew into a boom town and the boom was vastly inflated during the years when the DEW Line was being built. Hundreds of Eskimos from Baffin Island and other parts of the North were encouraged to come to Frobisher by the Canadian government. As late as 1960 government officials were indulging in extravagant prophecies that Frobisher would become the first true city in the North American Arctic. Government architects even drew up plans for high-rise buildings to be built under the protection of a gigantic plastic dome. But the advent of jet aircraft that had no need to stop for refuelling soon rendered the great airport obsolete. Like all communities based on a single industry, Frobisher Bay was terribly vulnerable and when its industry failed the community was doomed. However, there was this difference between Frobisher Bay and, say, a dying southern mining town: the Eskimo people of Frobisher Bay had nowhere else to go. They could not return to the ancestral life on the land, for they had changed from a hunting-and-trapping existence to an approximation of our artificial society. The South did not want them for they were less well adapted to our world than immigrants from Italy or Germany. They became, and now remain, truly displaced people. In 1967 the population of Frobisher Bay was composed of about five hundred whites, almost all of them transients, and eleven hundred Eskimos. The only available employment was in working for the government but all the key jobs, as well as most of the minor ones, were the prerogatives of white men and women. Government administrative personnel filled the gigantic building built by the United States to house its Strategic Air Command headquarters. One of the very few independent businesses operated by Eskimos anywhere in the Canadian Arctic, Inuk Limited, had as its sole remaining function the provision of janitor services for government buildings! The Eskimos of Frobisher Bay said, with bitter irony, that *they* did not need the Department of Northern Development nearly as much as the Department of Northern Development needed *them* – to justify its employment of so many teachers, administrators, maintenance men, social workers and sundry other bodies – all from southern Canada.

Frobisher Bay in 1967 was almost totally a welfare settlement. Despite the huge amounts of money that have been spent on it, it is a town without a reason to exist and it has no hope of a future – unless a miracle takes place. Canada's first arctic city has become a monument to stupidity and bureaucratic futility; but, unlike most monuments, its basic material is human clay instead of granite. It is a frightening symbol of the failure of Canada and Canadians to comprehend the reality of the North and to act accordingly. It is a place of ruin, a shabby, shoddy limbo filled with the wreckage of many broken lives.

The story is not quite so black elsewhere on the Icy Mountain coast. At the Padloping Islands, Broughton Island, Pangnirtung, and Clyde Inlet – all on the east coast of Baffin – there are communities that are still able to make some sort of living from the sea and from the land. They are peopled by the offspring of whalers and Eskimos, who are as tough and competent a people as are to be found anywhere. But they too are in rapid transition. Their children go to school and when they emerge from the system they will not be able to return to the land and the old ways, nor will they wish to do so. They will want, as some of them have already tried to tell us, to become part of our world while living in their own. To achieve this goal they must have assistance from men and women of the South who will really *live* among them – men and women with faith in the northern lands and the courage to build lives there. There are few such southern Canadians. At each of the settlements named above, the white population (apart from the Roman Catholic missionaries, who cling for a lifetime to their northern parishes) consists chiefly of a handful of governmental employees and Hudson's Bay Company staff, few of whom have any real intention of staying in the country or of making it their permanent home. I know of only one exception.

He is Ross Peyton at Pangnirtung, which has an Eskimo population of about six hundred. Here in one of the most spectacularly beautiful settings in the world, under the loom of the Pangnirtung Fiord mountains, Peyton is attempting to build a way of life for himself and his family. He operates a small store; he reloads ammunition for Eskimo hunters; he runs a movie projector and does many other things – but in everything he does he acts as a man who intends to remain here all his life as a *member* of the community. He is not at Pangnirtung to make a stake and then get out – a fact that used to puzzle the Eskimos, who had never met a man like him before. He spends at least half his time working with the people. He has established a handicraft co-operative for them. He has fought hard to persuade the government to build a tanning plant for seal skins here – and he has lost. In 1965 the Eskimos at "Pang" took eleven thousand seals, the skins of which could all have been used locally in the manufacture of handicrafts if there had been any way to tan them properly.

The large commercial organizations dislike "free traders." The government looks at them askance for they not fit into the bureaucratic mould. Peyton is a man who does not give up easily but when I visited him I could feel his frustration and sense the beginning of despair.

Frobisher Bay is moribund and the communities of the east coast are poised on the edge of dissolution, but the northern tip of Baffin Island shows signs of activity of the sort that appeals to the "think big" imagination of so many southern Canadians. In 1966 there were two small Eskimo communities at the top of the island, Pond Inlet and Arctic Bay, both barely surviving on the old hunting-and-trapping economy. However, a few miles inland from nearby Milne Inlet, at Mary's River, one of the richest potential iron mines in the world has been discovered. Millions of tons of ore have been proven, of such a degree of richness that neither concentration nor "beneficiation" is required – the ore can be fed straight into the blast furnace. Murray Watts, the old-time prospector who discovered the Mary's River ore body and who has been promoting it ever since, has raised and spent over a million dollars to build three airfields and more than forty miles of road from the mine site to tide-water. Several great mining consortiums, mostly foreign, have financial interests in this find but they are cautious about investing the requisite capital to start the mine producing. They feel that the short shipping season and the distance to European markets may not allow them sufficient profit. Watts believes he has the answer in the

Arctic fox
– drawn from nature by J. W. Audubon

"Spring came with the rapidity and violence of a summer thunder storm. Each day the snow around my tent retreated at least a dozen feet into the valleys below. The exposed gravel and dead moss steamed away like an over-anxious kettle. It was a queer thing to see and I felt as if I were sitting on the summit of a frozen world that, inexplicably, and with an unbelievable swiftness, had decided to collapse and melt away. Every hollow and low-lying spot harboured a freshet that quickened and murmured without pause for rest even during the brief twilight period that passed for night. The lake ice began to rock before my eyes. The shining surfaces turned leaden, dulled and fractured into countless millions of tiny, separate rods that were held upright and in place only by their mutual pressure on one another. Within a matter of days the sterile, unbreathing land of winter breathed deeply and its breath was that of a strong woman in the grip of passion."
– The People of the Deer, 1952

Walrus and young; *by an 18th century artist*

use of 500,000-ton bulk-ore freighters escorted by government icebreakers which would need to make only a few trips each summer in order to carry away an entire winter's stockpile of ore. Such ships were already being built in Japan in 1966. But the big companies would like the Canadian government to provide a large part of the risk capital to ensure their profits, and it is not inconceivable that it will do just that.

What the development of Mary's River and associated ore resources (there is a huge potential base-metal mine at Arctic Bay) means in terms of human beings is not yet clear. It may well be that far northern mines such as these will be so highly mechanized that they will require only a handful of technicians to operate them. If this proves to be so, they will be of little benefit to the people who now live in the North, and will do little to attract southern Canadians northward on a permanent basis. There seems to be some doubt that the money provided by our government in assistance funds will benefit anyone except the mine owners and their investors. It is at least a possibility that the removal of the non-renewable resources of the North will not mean development of the North, but only exploitation of it.

The full mineral resources of the Icy Mountains have not yet even been properly examined, let alone assessed. Flying north the length of Baffin Island one can see exposures of iron formation almost everywhere. Base-metal outcrops are nearly as abundant. When it becomes profitable to mine these and the as-yet-unknown mineral resources of east Baffin, Devon and the higher islands, we will have the opportunity to make this vast region an integral part of the nation – or we can treat it like an alien land to be high-graded and then abandoned. That choice is ours.

"The most fascinating animal in the North is the arctic wolf. The largest members of their species (an old male may weigh 160 lbs.), they come in all shades from black to white and they vary as much in individual personality as they do in colour. Highly intelligent, well-organized socially, and pre-eminently civilized in their behaviour, they deserve better than the persecution of poison, gun and trap. Harmless to man (there is not a single authentic case of a wolf in Canada ever having attacked a human being) they serve a vital role in the balance of nature. Despite this known fact, they have been made the scapegoat for many of our blunders in 'conservation'. It is easier to blame the wolf for the decrease in caribou, muskox and other such than to admit the blame ourselves. Having spent several months living close to a wild arctic wolf family, I conclude that the wolf is far less savage, wasteful, brutal and bestial than is man himself."
— Farley Mowat, 1967.

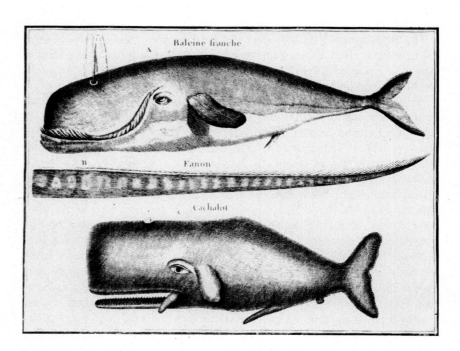

Herman Melville's "Moby Dick" was a cachalot (toothed whale, lower drawing). Whales must surface to breathe but some can stay under for an hour.

TRAVELLING NORTH

The true magnitude of the North is not to be measured in miles but in terms of our ability to conquer space and distance. Modern Canadians travel to and across it in jet planes, fast Diesel ships and snow-mobiles – even in sixty-knot Hovercraft – but are still appalled by its vastness. Yet, in the time it takes to fly from Montreal to Baffin Island, the men in these fishing vessels fighting the Labrador ice in 1864 would have been lucky to make ten miles. Although the North was virtually infinite to these men, it could not daunt their will.

HMS Alert *in the ice at Cape Sheridan in 1875: no ship has ever wintered further north (lat. 82° 30' N) and only one modern icebreaker has pushed closer to the Pole.* Alert *eventually became a buoy in the St. Lawrence.*

WINTER

SUMMER

A great voyage to the high ice

Through almost ten centuries ships have brought white men to the Canadian North, and have maintained them there. "Wooden ships and iron men" battled the ice from the days of Erik The Red who, in a fragile 80-ton sailing craft called a *knorr*, crossed from Greenland to Baffin Island in 982. During the 16th and 17th centuries much punier and less seaworthy ships were constantly daring the ice-laden seas. Martin Frobisher reached south Baffin Island in 1576 with the *Gabriel* and the *Michael* – tiny 20-tonners. John Davis' *Moonshine* was only 35-tons. The famous *Discovery* that carried Henry Hudson, William Baffin, George Weymouth and many others to the North was a bluff-bowed little ship of 55 tons. The Hudson's Bay Company's first ship, *Nonsuch,* was a mere 43 tons. None of these was much bigger than a good-sized pleasure yacht of today. During the 18th and 19th centuries the northern waters became crowded with Scottish, Basque, Yankee and Dutch whalers. In the later decades of the 1800's steam-auxilliary power came to the North, leading to the record-breaking voyage of the *Alert* and *Discovery* (a name-sake ship of 378 tons) in the Sir George Nares' expedition.

HMS Discovery, *with the Nares' polar expedition of 1875-76, chose a wintering place in Lady Franklin Sound, north Ellesmere Island. This (and the matching photo below) were taken by the paymaster of the ship.*

Exactly the same scene, in summer. Scurvy broke out in the .expedition and, when Alert returned through the Robeson Channel (between Ellesmere and Greenland), both ships set a course for Baffin Bay and England.

In Summer, a highway upon the waters

The year: 1900. The place: Great Slave Lake. Rowing their heavy boats, these Dogrib Indians could travel up to 20 miles a day and could require six weeks to get from their trapping camps to the nearest Hudson's Bay Co. trading post.

The women, as always, did the heaviest work. These Eskimos (below) in a big skin-covered umiak carry the camp gear to a new site while the menfolk lead the way in the light kayaks. Two husky women stood to handle each huge oar.

At break-up, a fur trader's canoe is manhandled toward opening water on the Slave River. In 1916, one trader covered an amazing 14,000 miles.

In Winter, tracks on the frozen sea

Men could cover prodigious distances with sleds and dogs – but it took a lot of time. Travelling Eskimo-style, the explorer Stefansson covered about 5000 miles through the arctic islands . . . in three years. Eskimos of the Keewatin plains thought nothing of a thousand-mile round trip to visit the trading post at Churchill. Space and distance held no terrors for these people. Coral Harbour Eskimos (below) set out from Southampton Island on a ten-day trip for seal.

The sled was in use before the discovery of the wheel, and it is still the carry-all of the Arctic. This heavy model freights furs fifty years ago.

The great sternwheelers brought life and legend to the North

The homely home-made Boston plied a stretch of the 2,500 mile Mackenzie, in her day an ultra-modern successor to the canoe and York boat. Sir Alexander Mackenzie first travelled down the waterway to the Beaufort Sea in 1789.

The freeze-up of 1901 found four of the Yukon's steam boats tied up in the shipyards at Dawson (and another a-building). These sternwheelers consumed a cord of wood an hour and stacks of fuel marked the riverbanks.

Where the Yukon narrowed into the maelstrom of Miles Canyon, the North's first railroad was born. A wooden tramway for horsedrawn wagons, it portaged cargo for five miles around White Horse and Squaw Rapids.

*Even a railroad was
lured north by the gold
of the fabulous Klondike*

Mountainous snowdrifts (above) have
always been accepted hazards on the White
Pass and Yukon Railway, running from
tidewater at Skagway (Alaska) to Whitehorse (Yukon), across the ferocious St.
Elias Range. Begun in 1898, the track was
rushed to completion in two years by
35,000 workers. By White Horse Rapids,
the right-of-way was carved out of solid
rock and high cliffs were blown apart by
dynamite. Soon, travellers rode in comfort
where thousands of horses — and more than
two hundred men — had died enroute.

Grades are so steep over the White Pass that five locomotives haul the narrow-guage trains across the divide.
Passengers are at times asked to get out and walk. For
three decades this was the only line into the North;
now, other lines reach Pine Point on the rim of Great
Slave Lake, and Churchill, on the Hudson Bay shore.

Construction steel was too expensive, and too difficult
to ship into the Yukon, so the early bridges were built
of wood. Culvert crossings like this one were often
washed out during spring floods but the road crews
could build a new one in a single day. The company
now has eight locomotives on the 110-mile track.

Horses and Huskies: The North creates its own conveyance

Model T, owned by a miner who struck it rich in the Klondike, was dubbed the "Red Devil". The dogs were not impressed.

The Overland Stage ready to set out from Whitehorse to Dawson City at the turn of the century. For five days, in forty-below weather, it crossed the Yukon, stopping every 22 miles at a roadhouse to change horses and feed the coon-skinned passengers with roast caribou and blueberry pie. The baggage allowance was 75 pounds for each person.

A tractor-drawn "cat train" loads in Yellowknife. Ordinary trailer trucks, led by a snow plow, can travel on packed snow.

Thin-skinned pioneer planes braved the blizzards

On the first flight into the North-West Territories this Imperial Oil Junkers was one of two that landed at Fort Simpson in the winter of 1920-21. Both planes smashed their propellors but were safely flown south with substitute props made on the spot. In 1929 bush pilot "Punch" Dickins became the first Canadian airman to cross the Arctic Circle.

This forlorn Fairchild FC2-W2, flown to the arctic coast by Matt Berry, was snowbound at Coppermine. Based on Edmonton Airport, daring pilots were soon flying discovery and mercy missions into areas once almost inaccessible. One flier located three starving men in a single igloo in the empty tundra.

The first airmail reaches Fort Resolution, Great Slave Lake, in January, 1929. When World War 1 ace "Wop" May flew in the first mails, philatelists swamped him with four tons of letters. Prospectors chartered the flimsy planes to get in to likely areas; Gilbert LaBine spotted Canada's first uranium mine at Great Bear Lake by this method.

Since 1941, this war-time Martin bomber (and two others like it) has lain in Million Dollar Valley, south-east Yukon. Empty fuselages now, they were put down by a squadron leader who lost his way during a flight to Alaska. Canadian pilot Russ Baker flew his Junkers in to pick up the 24 stranded aircrew. The fast, safe aircraft of today have shrunk the region to a manageable size. In 1966, a new trans-polar service connecting Montreal and Moscow was inaugurated.

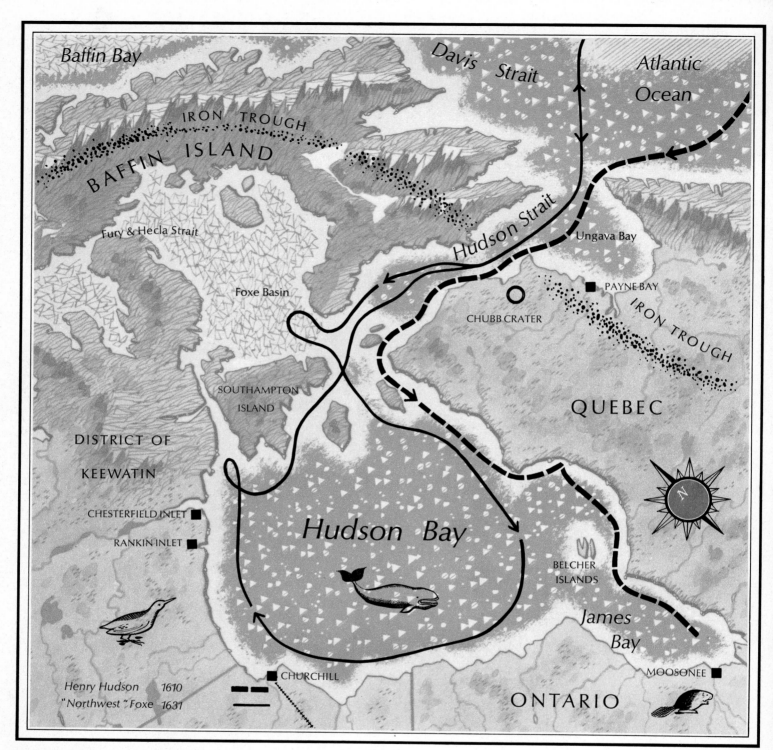

Baffin Bay

Davis Strait

Atlantic Ocean

IRON TROUGH

BAFFIN ISLAND

Fury & Hecla Strait

Foxe Basin

Hudson Strait

Ungava Bay

CHUBB CRATER

PAYNE BAY

IRON TROUGH

QUEBEC

SOUTHAMPTON ISLAND

DISTRICT OF KEEWATIN

CHESTERFIELD INLET

RANKIN INLET

Hudson Bay

BELCHER ISLANDS

James Bay

CHURCHILL

Henry Hudson 1610
"Northwest" Foxe 1631

MOOSONEE

ONTARIO

The Canadian Sea

5

Although most of us are aware that Canada is bounded on the north, east and west by three oceans, few Canadians realize that there is a mighty sea right in the middle of our country. Part of the difficulty is that, like the range that includes the Torngats and the Icy Mountains, it has no name. We call the largest part of it Hudson Bay (although it is not correctly a bay at all); but this is by no means the whole sea. Canada's nameless inland ocean (the name Canadian Sea is my own) is composed of Hudson Bay, James Bay, Foxe Basin, Hudson Strait and Ungava Bay, and it is one of the world's two greatest inland seas – the other being the Mediterranean Sea, which is only a third larger.

The Mediterranean Sea is oriented east and west. The Canadian Sea runs thirteen hundred miles from north to south and is nearly six hundred miles across at its widest point. Nobody can be certain how such a gigantic body of salt water became trapped in the interior of the continent. One explanation is that the Canadian Sea marks the site of a monstrous icecap from the recent Pleistocene epoch – an icecap on a par with the Greenland cap and which, like the Greenland cap, grew so weighty that it depressed the earth's crust to form a titanic bowl the centre of which filled with salt water from the Atlantic after the retreat of the glacier. The remainder of the bowl now forms a drainage basin of almost a million and a half square miles and is fed by the waters of scores of great rivers including the Nelson, Saskatchewan, Thelon, Churchill, Fort George and Moose. In keeping with the icecap theory is the fact that the floor of the Canadian Sea is rebounding at what, in terms of geological time, is a startling rate. Thus the Canadian Sea has shrunk by something like half its area during the past ten thousand years; its coastal plains for as much as two hundred miles inland clearly show that they were formerly sea bottom. Seen from the air the west coast of Southampton Island appears to be almost as sterile as if it had just emerged from the sea and hundreds of old sand and gravel beaches overlap each other for many miles into the interior. Camp sites of the Dorset Eskimo culture which were situated on water-lapped beaches three thousand years ago now sit high and dry forty or fifty feet above sea level and as much as five miles inland.

The Canadian Sea has other peculiarities. Perhaps the oddest is a great semi-circular bite out of the southeast coast of Hudson Bay. Curving south

Spirit of the Fisherman.
Engraving on stone by Inukjurakju.

Northern peoples of Eskimoan lineage are amongst the most artistic of the world's races. In Canada they have demonstrated their skills in scores of ways and there seems to be no limit to their ingenuity or to the mediums in which they can work. In Siberia the related Chukchees have produced such internationally known writers as Yuri Ritkheu (fifteen novels translated into thirty languages) and, once they escape from illiteracy, Canadian Eskimos will doubtless do as well.

Birds and Woman's Face.
Stone engraving by Kenojuak.

*"One morning I was awakened from an
uneasy sleep by the mad laughter of
many voices chuckling in zany mirth.
I flung open the door and found myself
staring into the eyes of half a hundred
disembodied heads. The heads were
chicken like, but stained dull red as if by
the life blood of the bodies they had
been parted from. I stared at the weird
visitors and they stared back and laughed
until the whole valley rang with sound.
I flung a piece of ice at one and the whole
flock suddenly took flight. As they cleared
the ground, their trim white bodies that
had been invisible against the snow came
into view and I knew them then for
ptarmigan, the white partridge of the
Arctic."*

– Farley Mowat, 1952.

from Portland Promontory to Cape Jones, the coast forms a precise geometric arc, part of a circle which if projected to completion would have a diameter of about three hundred miles. The missing part of the circle lies under the waters of Hudson Bay, and roughly in the centre of the circle there is a peculiar complex of stringy, curved islands known as the Belchers. They display a pattern that can be visualized if one imagines what glacial and water erosion might do to one of the great upthrust mounds of a lunar crater. The Belcher Islands are immensely rich in iron and comparison of their basic material shows a resemblance to the composition of some iron meteorites. A few miles off shore from the landward curve, and precisely paralleling it, is an almost continuous row of linear islands – the Nastapokas. These too are peculiar, and can most easily be described as what the outer ridge of lunar crater could look like if exposed to earth-type erosion. The presence of the nearby Chubb crater in Ungava – one of the largest recognized meteorite craters in the world – does nothing to invalidate the possibility that southern Hudson Bay may have been the site of one of the most stupendous meteorite strikes in the history of our planet.

The Canadian Sea is entered from the Atlantic through a rock-toothed gap between the north Labrador mountains and southern Baffin Island. The mouth is followed by a long, southeast-northwest throat known as Hudson Strait. Just inside the mouth Ungava Bay sags south like a huge goitre. The throat opens, between Cape Dorset on Baffin Island and Cape Wolstenholme on Ungava Peninsula, into the ·Canadian Sea proper. To the south lies Hudson Bay. To the north lies the shallow, usually ice-filled expanse of Foxe Basin, bordered by the saturated lowland plains of west Baffin Island and east Melville Peninsula. Foxe Basin is partly separated from Hudson Bay by the triangular mass of Southampton Island and by the lesser barriers of Coats and Mansel islands. James Bay forms an appendix at the south end of Hudson Bay and both it and Hudson Bay are surrounded by lowlands that often approach the condition of flooded bogs.

In the extreme northwest corner of Foxe Basin a narrow channel – Fury and Hecla Strait – provides a back door out of the Canadian Sea to the westward. Up to our time this channel has proved useless for navigation since it is often choked with ice. However, modern icebreakers would have little difficulty keeping it open if we so desired, thereby providing a passage from the Canadian Sea to the waters of the western Arctic. Just south and west of Southampton, Chesterfield Inlet and Baker Lake together form a sea-route extending two hundred miles west-northwest into the heart of the great Keewatin tundra. First explored in 1761 and 1762 by Captain William Christopher and Moses Norton of the Hudson's Bay Company, this mighty inlet will admit ocean-going ships of considerable tonnage.

If we didn't have the Canadian Sea it would be a good idea to dig it because it provides direct access to salt water for a vast portion of the interior of Canada. Incredible as it may seem, the distance from Churchill, on the *west side* of Hudson Bay and lying very near the geographic centre of Canada, to Liverpool in England, is about the same as the sea distance from Montreal to Liverpool! *It is in the north that Canada is closest to the other continents of the northern hemisphere.*

This basic fact of geography was very much a reality to early European explorers and in part explains why the Canadian Sea once played a most important role in the history of this country. The first Europeans to reach it – so far as we know – were the Norse working their way down the Baffin coast from Cape Dyer during the decades after Erik the Red discovered

Baffin Island. The Norse were great seamen and like those who followed them were able to understand the significance of the massive tidal stream which flows into and out of the gaping mouth of Hudson Strait. They called the place *Gingungagap* – meaning a strait leading to another ocean. In due course they explored it. They were looking for good hunting lands and these they found in Ungava Bay, which became known to them as *Skuggifiord*. Perhaps as early as 1100 they began to colonize the west coast of Ungava.

How do we know this? Partly because the Icelanders retained a body of sagas that preserve fragments of the Skuggifiord story, but mainly due to the work of an archaeologist named Thomas Lee from Laval University's *Centre d'Etudes Nordiques*. Although ruins that were obviously not Eskimo were found at Payne Bay on the west Ungava coast in 1957, it was left to Lee to investigate them some ten years later. He found a sequence of structures dating back several hundred years. He found great round cairns set up at the mouth of the Payne River that pre-date our colonial period and were apparently intended as leading marks for skippers trying to navigate those dangerous waters (the tidal range in Payne Bay is more than forty-five feet). On outlying islets he and other investigators have found ancient eider-duck nesting shelters made of stone. Eskimos are not known to have built such things, but early Scandinavian peoples did so. Lee has examined (and so have I) a great ruin that was found by archaeologists in 1956 but not dug. It is the remains of a stone-and-turf-walled structure some eighty-five feet long and more than thirty feet wide with slightly curved outer walls and traces of at least three internal partitions. It is identifiable in all salient features with the Norse *skala* or long hall of the twelfth century and earlier.

The entire west coast of Ungava Bay is littered with cairns, house ruins and other structures which are not reasonably attributable to any known Eskimo cultures. However, Lee's major discovery is an inland village site where he has found a row of square stone ruins, neatly floored with stone paving. A nearby pond had been dammed and crossed by a causeway eight feet wide. At one end of this village "street" stands a structure having such a close similarity to twelfth-century Greenlandic churches that its origin can hardly be in doubt.

Lee has just begun his work – it will take a decade to examine even the known ruins – but already it is apparent that the west Ungava Bay shores harboured a major European – or European derived – settlement of great antiquity (by North American standards). The question of what happened to the vanished inhabitants is already partially answered. From the evidence of the preliminary excavations it seems likely that a Norse culture in the region gradually lost its distinctive features and merged with a local Eskimo culture. This process may have taken a long time, but it was inevitable: even the Norse in Greenland itself disappeared in this way when contact with Europe was lost during the fourteenth century. The latest ruins in the series seem to demonstrate the existence of a people who were not quite Eskimo, but who were no longer European.

Ungava Bay is a backwater now, but it may one day recover its lost importance. Running north from near the height of land in Quebec-Labrador a belt of iron formation extends to and up the west coast of Ungava Bay and right up the spine of Baffin Island. This iron trough may well be the greatest occurrence of iron ore on the surface of the globe. It is already being mined at Schefferville in mid-Ungava and at Wabush and Labrador

Eagle carrying man.
Stone engraving by Pudlo.

Eskimo family.
Engraving by Kiakshuk.

Old ways of the white man change slowly in the North but one hopeful move in recent years has been the Church of England's new policy of ordaining native preachers to replace missionaries from abroad. In 1966, the church had five Eskimo ministers in the Arctic and was preparing to ordain several more.

City. But it is easier to reach this trough of ore from Ungava Bay than from the St. Lawrence, and one day the existing, but undeveloped holdings of Cyrus Eaton and of Krupp in the Fort Chimo and Leaf River areas of Ungava will undoubtedly be exploited, as will nearby findings farther north of zinc, lead and silver. And the Bay has another latent value: its tides. At Leaf Bay the spring tides run as high as sixty-four feet – as high as any in the world – and they could readily be harnessed in Leaf Basin to produce millions of horse-power of electricity. Base-metal mines and cheap power close together could mean a mining-smelting complex on Ungava Bay and settlements with permanence as opposed to the here-today-gone-tomorrow towns that spring up and die away at mines whose raw product is exported direct to the "outside".

The early Norse explorations of the Canadian Sea were never entirely forgotten, although the people themselves disappeared. It is possible that around 1470 a Scandinavian named Johan Scolvus piloted a Danish expedition into Hudson Bay. In 1508 Sebastian Cabot reached, and may have entered, Hudson Strait. The irrepressible Martin Frobisher sailed into the strait in 1578 – by accident, for he was trying to get back to the bay now named after him. Then, in 1610, the man whose name the strait and bay now bear sailed west, poked about in Ungava Bay, cleared Hudson Strait, sailed almost to the foot of Hudson Bay where he wintered and then was cast adrift by a mutinous crew. But Henry Hudson had made his mark.

With the Canadian Sea officially discovered by the English, a rush began. Thomas Button, Robert Bylot, "North-West" Foxe, Thomas James, and others hastened to the new sea all hoping to find a passage out of it to the northwest. There was one stranger in their midst. In 1619 the King of Denmark sent out a man named Jens Munk, not merely to discover the Northwest Passage, but to reclaim by settlement the lands the Scandinavians had discovered and upon which the English were now trespassing. Munk's story is a grisly one. He and his men lacked the old Norsemen's ability to become a part of the northern world and, by the spring of 1620, sixty-one men had died of scurvy, leaving Munk and two other survivors, all deathly sick, to make their way back to Denmark in a leaking tub of a ship.

After the Munk disaster the Danes withdrew from the game, but the inland ocean continued to draw new explorers. By 1660, two French fur traders, Chouart Des Groseilliers and Radisson, grasped the real importance of the Canadian Sea: that it provided by far the most direct ocean route between Europe and the fur-producing centre of the new continent. Failing to persuade their own people of this fact, they turned to the court of Charles II. They persuaded English merchants to outfit an expedition that sailed in 1668. The voyage was so great a success that in 1670 a charter was granted to the Governor and Company of Adventurers of England Trading into Hudson's Bay. It is a date to remember. From that time forward the inland ocean became (though not without sundry fights with the French and later with free traders) the private lake of the Hudson's Bay Company and the entrepôt from which that company spread its trade tenacles all through the North American west and north. The salient fact that Chouart Des Groseilliers and Radisson first comprehended became the central principle behind the operations of the company through the next two centuries – and it paid big dividends. Indeed it would pay them still if the true value of the Canadian Sea had not been forgotten by modern Canada.

When the English first reached the shores of the Canadian Sea its coasts were already well populated. From Churchill south around James Bay and

How Eskimo art came out of the Arctic into the nation's living rooms

When Toronto artist James Houston (*right:* a page from his Arctic sketchbook) visited the Hudson Bay area in 1947, he brought back some samples of Eskimo carving in soapstone. They found eager buyers and soon he had established a thriving craft centre at Cape Dorset, Baffin Island, where he was later appointed Civil Administrator. With his family, he lived there for nine years. In travelling 60,000 miles in the Arctic, he usually sheltered at night in an igloo which he could construct in 40 minutes. After a trip to Japan, Houston introduced print making to the Eskimos. He lives in the U.S. now and the art colony at Cape Dorset continues to thrive under the guidance of Terry Ryan.

Houston is a member of the Eskimo Art Commission which ensures first-rate work is shipped for sale.

Ice fishing, 1960.

Baffin Island, 1963.

At Grinnell River, N.W.T., 1965.

The Hunt.
Engraving by Juanisialu.

"When I first met Father Steinmann, the prickly, no-nonsense Roman Catholic priest, he as good as told me to go to the devil because he disagreed with books I had written about the Eskimos. When I refused to go, he grinned and took me into his house where we talked until dawn. But first he dug out an ancient Colt revolver and a two-foot snow knife. Giving me the knife, and keeping the revolver himself, he announced in a bellowing, gravelly voice that he was ready to join battle. Disagreeing with government policy, mission policy, and most other 'northern' policies, Steinmann does not hesitate to state his views to all comers. To him northern development means people; and the Eskimos at Povungnituk for whom he has laboured unstintingly over the years, admire and respect him greatly . . . though continuing to worship in the Church of England."
— Farley Mowat, 1966

Blocking the Seal Hole.
by Siasi Atitu.

north to Fort George, Indians of Algonkian stock lived and hunted. In the vicinity of Churchill the great Chipewyan nation reached the inland sea. North of the Chipewyans a quarter of a million square miles of tundra were occupied, if sparsely, by several thousand Caribou Eskimos whose only contact with the outer world was along the west coast of Hudson Bay. Other tribes of Eskimos occupied the east coast of Hudson Bay, Ungava Peninsula, both sides of Ungava Bay and Atlantic Labrador. Around Foxe Basin the seal- and walrus-hunting Central Eskimos lived in large numbers.

But things have changed. On the east coast of Hudson Bay there are now only three real communities; Great Whale River, Port Harrison and Povungnituk. Of those only P.O.V. (as Povungnituk is familiarly known) seems viable. It is a hopeful place largely because of the indefatigable and lusty efforts of a priest of the Oblate order, Father André Steinmann, who labours not merely to save souls (he has only a handful of parishioners) but to assist the Eskimos to find a way of life that will allow them to become part of the modern world. He has had a remarkable success, and the existence of the Povungnituk Eskimo Co-operative, which earns as much as $200,000 a year exporting hand-crafted goods and carvings to the south, is largely due to his efforts.

There is another example of this kind of dedicated work at Cape Dorset on the southwest coast of Baffin. There a young Torontonian named Terry Ryan is manager of the West Baffin Island Co-operative. Ryan is actually a salaried employee of the local Eskimos. He has built a house of his own, has married a nurse and intends to make Cape Dorset his permanent home. With his assistance the Dorset co-op has become world famous as an artists' colony – not, be it noted, as an *Eskimo* artists' colony. The Dorset artists are artists first and Eskimos incidentally.

A third example of a committed southerner in the North was to be found at Rankin Inlet on the west coast of Hudson Bay, where a nickel mine was operated for five years. (It closed abruptly in 1962, when the richest ore had been exhausted.) Under the aegis of a rough-and-ready manager named Andy Easton this mine became a training ground for Eskimos and, before it closed, was run almost entirely by the native people. Like Steinmann, Ryan and Peyton, Easton did no more than give the Eskimos the opportunity to work for a living while they learned our skills and methods. The Eskimos themselves did the rest. But then the mine closed down. Rankin Inlet, with a population of several hundred Eskimos drawn to it by the mine, began to die. The Department of Northern Development did what it could to revive the place, but it is largely due to the efforts of one of the Department's own people, Bob Williamson, who resigned the service, that there is a new spirit in Rankin and a new hope. A young French-Canadian couple moved in to show the people how to make ceramic sculpture. A German immigrant set up a pilot canning plant which produces a dazzling variety of northern culinary delicacies for the carriage trade down south. Both of these are D.N.D. projects and credit for them must go to the Department – but if Bob Williamson and his wife had not had the courage to give up a safe job, settle down in a permanent house in Rankin, and rally the baffled people to fight for a future, it is unlikely that Rankin would today be more than another welfare camp.

Just south of Rankin Inlet is an example of what might have happened. At Eskimo Point in 1966 there were four hundred people and there was no Williamson, Steinmann, Ryan or Peyton. There was no work. There was almost nothing for the people to do except sit about the one-room wooden prefabs supplied by the government and live on the dole. The fate of Eskimo Point is, unfortunately, all too typical of the majority of northern settlements. Rankin, P.O.V., and Cape Dorset are exceptions.

Around the shores of the Canadian Sea live about thirty-five hundred survivors of the original population of Indians and Eskimos. Apart from the people at P.O.V., Rankin (and its satellite, Whale Cove) and Dorset, they have little hope and, in reality, they no longer really belong to their own land. Nevertheless they could and would rebuild their own lives and build a vital new part of Canada into the bargain if we would help them find a new *raison d'être*, and show them the way out of the blind alley into which we have misguidedly herded them.

Meanwhile the Canadian Sea is teeming with unrealized possibilities. Churchill is a prime example. It has been continuously inhabited by Europeans for more than two and a half centuries, but it was not until 1929, after prolonged agitation by Westerners who saw what Radisson and others had seen, that a railway was finally completed from The Pas to Churchill, where a large grain elevator and marine terminal were also constructed. It was intended that western grain should be shipped to Europe by the short northern route. Grain *was* and *is* being shipped, but it is hardly more than a trickle – a gesture. With only minor additions to its handling facilities Churchill could ship twenty times its present volume of grain and other products, and could receive an equivalent amount of incoming freight from Europe. Modern navigation aids, aircraft ice patrols, and the new ice-breakers of the Department of Transport could keep this northern sea route open nearly twice as long each year as it is at present. But it appears that little if anything is being done to realize the dream, primarily because of opposition from southern interests, including a major railroad, Quebec and Ontario ports, and the American and Canadian supporters of the St. Lawrence Seaway. (Freight rates for grain to Montreal were lowered substantially on completion of the Hudson Bay railway.) Thus today Churchill remains essentially what it was in the early 1930's – a decrepit and lacklustre village that survives largely through government bounty and through a few small-scale opportunist activities carried on by a few hardy individuals. Comparable northern ports in the U.S.S.R. have become thriving cities while Churchill barely staggers on towards its hazy future.

The potential of the Canadian Sea as a waterway is almost limitless. There is no reason why Ontario could not have a salt-water port for deep-sea vessels on James Bay through which manufactured goods could be shipped direct to Europe by the shortest, cheapest route. A railroad from Great Slave Lake to Baker Lake via the Thelon plains (proposed and actually surveyed in 1900) would cost about two-thirds of what the recently built railroad to Great Slave Lake from northern Alberta cost the Canadian tax-payers. It would provide a deep-sea outlet for mineral products from over half a million square miles of the North as well as from the burgeoning mining region around Great Slave Lake itself. The day may come when refining plants and even industrial plants making use of the northern ores will give birth to large, permanent communities on the shores of the inland ocean. But until our thinking about northern development and our approach to economic methods have both altered considerably, it seems more likely that the Canadian Sea will remain a vague and frozen realm beyond our ken.

Loon.
Stone engraving by Davidialu.

Portrait of an Eskimo

"Hekwaw was a mountain of a man. His muscles bulged and flowed under the loose sleeves of his old parka. Sweat beaded up under his lank black hair then rolled down the oblique slant of his low forehead to run along the deep seams of his skin. His broad and sensuous mouth lay under the scraggy screen of a few dozen grizzled hairs that served as a moustache. It was a parody of a face, one that was surely meant for comedy but which had wild essential quality that restrained my desire to laugh. Here was deep intelligence where one might expect to see only brute instinct, and there was humour and good nature that belied the weathered hide crinkling, ape-like, on the brow and flat planed cheeks."

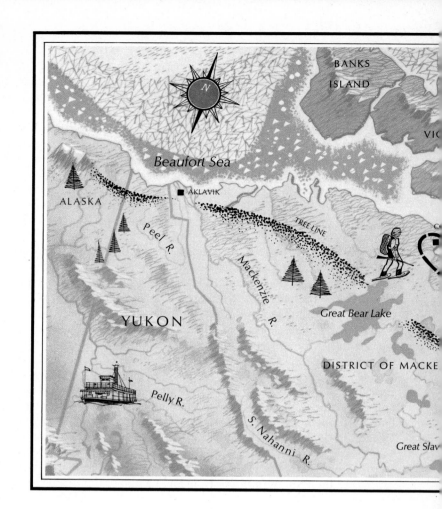

6

The Northern Prairie

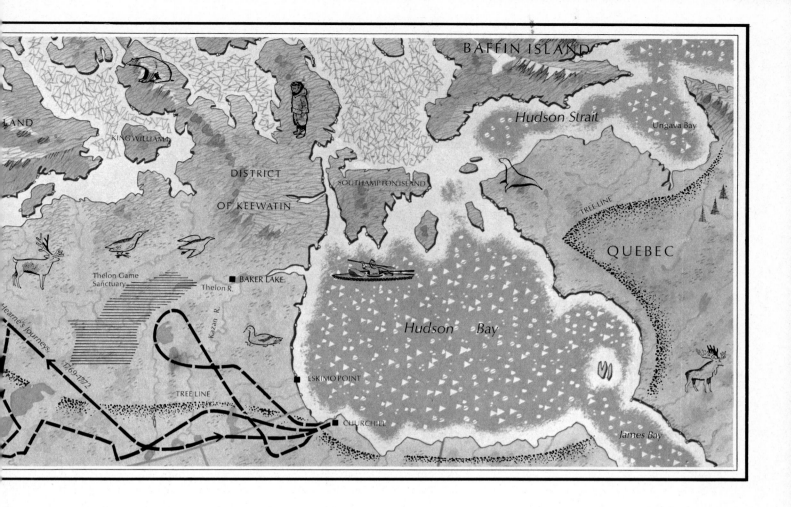

Hudson Strait

Ungava Bay

LAND

KING WILLIAM

DISTRICT

OF KEEWATIN

SOUTHAMPTON ISLAND

TREE LINE

QUEBEC

Thelon Game
Sanctuary

Thelon R.

■ BAKER LAKE

Kazan R.

Hudson   Bay

Hearne's Journeys

1769-1772

TREE LINE

ESKIMO POINT

■ CHURCHILL

James Bay

S prawled across the upper mainland of the North to both sides of
Hudson Bay lies a tremendous tract of tundra that for centuries has
been known to Europeans as the Barren Grounds, the Barren Lands,
or simply the Barrens. To the eastward the Barrens include the whole
of the Ungava Peninsula between Ungava Bay and Hudson Bay (plus a
narrow strip along the east shore of Ungava Bay). To the west they
form an immense triangle whose apex touches the Alaska-Yukon border
at the Beaufort Sea. The northern arm of the triangle extends eastward
fourteen hundred miles along the Arctic coast to the shores of the Canadian
Sea. The southern arm runs fourteen hundred miles southeast past Great
Bear Lake and past the east end of Great Slave Lake to Churchill in northern
Manitoba. The base of the triangle is the west coast of the Canadian Sea,
from Churchill six hundred miles north to Repulse Bay. This western
region is linked to the Ungava Barrens by a narrow coastal strip running
south and east from Churchill to the top of James Bay then north up the
east coast of Hudson Bay to Richmond Gulf.

The mainland Barrens of Canada embrace better than half a million
square miles of rolling, lake-dotted plains broken here and there by ranges
of old, worn-down hills. To an observer in a small aircraft droning for endless hours over its illimitable space, the tundra seems to be almost as much
a world of water as of land. Its lakes, ponds and rivers are beyond counting.
Seen from the air the land between appears to be dun-coloured, mono-

*When this drawing of curlews was made
in 1792, the birds were thick in the North.
By 1954 none had been seen for a decade;
recently a few birds have been identified.*

The Ptarmigan

The ptarmigan — a kind of grouse,
Lives in the Arctic with his spouse.
The ptarmigan is smart and perky
And tastes much better than a pturkey.
                                        — F.M.

The northern plains

"It is a place where curlews circle in a
white sky above icily transparent lakes.
It is a place where gaudy ground squirrels
whistle from the sandy casts of vanished
glacial rivers; where the dun-colored
summer foxes den, and lemmings dawdle
fattly in the thin sedges of the bogs. It is a
place where minute flowers blaze in
microcosmic revelry and where the
thrumming of insect wings asails the
greater beasts and sets them fleeing to
the bald ridge tops in search of a wind to
drive the unseen enemy away. It is a place
where the black muskox still stand four
square to the cautious feints of the white
wolves and where the shambling giant of
the land, the massive Barrens grizzly,
moves solitary and untouchable. And,
not long since, it was a place where the
caribou in unnumbered hordes could
inundate the land in one hot flow of life
that rose below one far horizon and
reached unbroken past the opposite one."

chromatic, apparently featureless, reaching to the horizon on all sides with an illusion of interminable monotony.

This is strictly an illusion. Look closer and the void of land and water becomes an intricate mosaic, varied and colourful. The multitudes of tundra ponds are shallow and reflect the pale northern skies in every shade of blue and violet or, discoloured by the organic stains of muskeg water, they become sepia, burnished copper, burning red or shimmering green. The numberless rivers run no straight courses but twist tortuously through chocolate-brown muskegs or between silver-grey ridges of stone and gravel (the moraines of the vanished glaciers) or compete in pattern-making with the meandering embankments of sandy eskers (the casts of dead rivers that once flowed under the melting ice sheet). Some eskers roam for hundreds of miles and bear a disconcerting resemblance to the constructions of a long-forgotten race of manic giants.

Viewed by a summer traveller on the ground the tundra gives the feeling of limitless space, intensified until one wonders if there can be any end to this terrestrial ocean whose waves are the rolling ridges. Perhaps nowhere else in the world, except far out at sea, does a man feel so naked and exposed. On the northern prairie it is as if the ceiling of the world no longer exists and no walls remain to close one in.

In winter this sea simile gains even greater weight, for then both land and water vanish, blending into one impassive sweep of frozen undulations that seems to have no limit and no shore.

The climate of the northern prairies is not so very different from that of their southern counterparts. Winter is longer on the tundra but not a great deal colder than on the Saskatchewan plains. Summer is shorter, but the sun shines throughout most of every twenty-four-hour period and during the long summer days the northern plains can become uncomfortably hot. Soil is scanty, but the long summer day helps make up for that and growth is fast and lush. As on the southern prairies, precipitation, both rain and snow, is light; but in the North where the soil is shallow, permafrost ever present and evaporation slow, this hardly matters.

Why these mighty plains should have been called "barren" is hard to understand. Even if the word is only intended to mean treeless, it is not valid. Along the entire southern fringe there are trees, small and stunted it is true, but trees. And scattered over the southern half of the northern prairies are islands of timber. One of these, on the Thelon River and almost dead centre in the plains, forms a timbered oasis forty or fifty miles in length with some single trees growing thirty feet in height. If "barren" is meant to mean barren of life it is a gross misnomer. True, in winter there is not much life to be seen, but in summer the tundra is vividly alive.

For the most part the land is covered with a rich carpet of mosses, lichens, grasses, sedges and dwarf shrubbery. The flowers are small, many of them minute, but they grow in fantastic abundance. Even on the naked ridges and on the frost-riven graveyards of broken stone that lie between some of the muskeg valleys, there is brilliant life; the rocks glow with the splashed kaleidoscope of lichens in a hundred shades.

Animate life is just as abundant. The innumerable ponds, muskegs and lakes are the breeding grounds for stupendous numbers of ducks, geese and wading birds. The dry tundra and the rock tundra is the habitat of the northern grouse called ptarmigan, and of innumerable other birds. Snowy owls nest on the grassy flats and rough-legged hawks and falcons share the pale sky with the uncompromising raven which, almost alone among arctic animals, refuses to change his colour when winter whiteness obliterates the world. The waters of the larger lakes (those that do not freeze to the bottom in winter) and, in summer, the rivers are full of white fish, lake trout (forty-pounders are not uncommon), suckers and a flamboyant and peculiar fish – a distant relative of the trout – called grayling.

Insects there are in quantity – a mixed blessing, for although it is pleasant to see butterflies and bumblebees it is not so pleasant to cope with the hordes of mosquitos and black flies that, particularly in the more southerly regions, can make life hell on windless days. Fortunately there are few totally windless days in the northern prairies and, in any case, the flies are not a great deal worse than they are in parts of the southern forest regions where Canadians delight to spend their summer holidays.

It is the mammals that dominate the land. During the peak periods of their cycles, short-tailed, mouse-like lemmings are so abundant that one can hardly walk across the sedge and moss without sending them scuttling clumsily from under foot. They provide the chief food of the white fox whose cycle of abundance is keyed to theirs. Lemmings know nothing about birth control. They breed so prolifically that every four or five years they literally eat and crowd themselves out of house and home and then must either die or migrate elsewhere – and such migrations are fatal for most of them.

Even squirrels live on the tundra – gaudy, orange-coloured ground squirrels that den in the sandy eskers or on dry gravel ridges, where the perpetual frost does not deny them entry to the ground.

The great white wolves of the tundra, once abundant, display an amiable curiosity, visiting human campsites to sit with cocked ears as they watch the inscrutable activities of men.

One of the most impressive of all the tundra beasts is the great brown bear called the Barren Ground Grizzly. Only a few decades ago this shambling giant roamed over most of mainland tundra west of Hudson Bay, but now, like so many other species that have roused our murderous appetites, he has become so rare as almost to be just a memory.

Equally strange is the muskox – a black, stolid beast that looks like a cross between a bull and a huge shaggy goat (actually it is related, distantly, to both). Slow and placid but armed with sweeping horns, the muskox have evolved the tactic of forming a hollow square when threatened. Because of their fine underlying wool the wildest winter weather cannot affect them. They have no real enemies save man, and in other times they called almost the entire tundra, both on the mainland and on the islands, home. But by the mid-twenties they had been almost exterminated, and it was chiefly through the persistence of an extraordinary man named W. H. B. Hoare, an ex-missionary who became the champion of the vanishing muskox, that the government in 1927 established a sanctuary for the shaggy beasts in the Thelon valley. Now the muskox are gradually increasing and may one day regain much of their lost territory.

By far the most impressive of all the tundra beasts is the caribou. Caribou have literally provided the lifeblood of the human residents of the northern plains and of the taiga since time immemorial. These cousins of the reindeer formerly existed in such huge herds that they approached in number the buffalo of the southern prairies and probably outnumbered any of the great herd beasts of Africa. When Europeans first arrived on the edge of the northern prairie there may have been as many as five million caribou. Caribou and their predators, chiefly wolves, and the native peoples had lived to-

Mystery surrounds the largest of all mainland arctic mammals—the hulking Barren Ground grizzly bear. Solitary and enigmatic, leaving footprints as big as pie plates, this shambling giant once roamed over most of the northern prairies west of Hudson Bay. Eskimos gave it a wide berth — not out of fear, for there is not a single record of a man being harmed by a grizzly in the Northwest Territories, but out of respect for a sagacious and mightily impressive fellow resident of the tundra. All that has changed. White men hunt the big bear because they fear him or covet his head and hide as a trophy and, in 1965, an open season was declared on the 500 remaining Barren Ground grizzlies. It seems likely that those little known giants of the tundra plains may soon become no more than a memory.

The Snowy Owl

The Snowy Owl, I've heard it said,
Lives on the entrails of the dead.
It loves to gorge on rotting bowel.
Which spoils it — as a table fowl.

— F.M.

"When full grown the muskox is as large as the middling size of English black cattle, but their legs are not so long; nor is their tail longer than a bear's, and it is entirely hid by the long hair of the rump. Their hair is very long, but the longest hair, particularly the bulls', is under the throat, extending from the chin to the lower part of the chest. It hangs down like a horse's mane inverted, and is fully as long."

— *Samuel Hearne,* Journey to the Northern Ocean, *1795.*

gether in balance for uncounted ages. We soon changed that. In 1949, after Ottawa had finally taken notice of the terrible destruction of these northern deer, an aerial survey showed that probably only about 650,000 remained alive. By 1955 there were estimated to be about 280,000. By 1960 there were estimated to be fewer than 200,000, most of them west of Hudson Bay. In the Ungava Barrens the caribou had virtually disappeared as early as 1920. It is only fair to add that recent estimates from both Ungava and Keewatin are higher. And indeed, there are indications that, under strict protection, the slide towards extinction may have been halted and even reversed. It is too soon to say whether we have acted in time.

Certainly the fur trade helped destroy the caribou. It turned the northern peoples from hunting meat for their own use to destroying animals wholesale in order to convert meat into bait and dog feed to trap more efficiently and also to provide the northern fur brigades of the trading companies with quantities of pemmican. High-powered repeating rifles accomplished what thousands of years of bow and arrow, deer corrals, spearing at river crossings and snaring, poor fawning seasons, and wolves had not been able to do – they broke the balance between man and beast. The destruction was greatly assisted by white trappers, some of whom killed as many as four hundred caribou a year for bait and dog feed; and by white prospectors who deliberately burned off millions of acres of caribou winter range inside the taiga in order to expose the native rock beneath. (In Quebec and Labrador forest fires have been a primary reason for the decimation of the herds.)

The destruction of the caribou was on the same scale as the destruction of the prairie buffalo. The northern deer had been so abundant that as late as 1900 herds which could only be described in terms of square miles still existed. There is a reliable record of a single herd seen in 1897 that consisted of more than two hundred thousand caribou.

When Samuel Hearne crossed the plains from Churchill to the Coppermine River in the late 1700's he found several thousand Indians, both in the taiga and on the tundra, living exclusively on caribou. When those other great explorers of the western tundras, J. B. and J. W. Tyrrell, entered Keewatin in 1893 there were approximately two thousand Eskimos in the interior who did not visit the sea coast and were exclusively a people of the deer. In Ungava, between 1830 and 1900, the Indians of the inland and, to a lesser extent, the Eskimos led lives predicated on caribou. By 1966 in the whole vast stretch of interior Keewatin there was *not one* resident Indian or Eskimo except at a single settlement, Baker Lake. The interior tundra of Ungava and the interior tundra regions of Mackenzie were also all-but empty of native peoples. The many and varied peoples of the deer across the breadth of the northern Canadian plains vanished with the caribou. Fewer than two score of the inland Eskimos still survive, most of them huddling in wooden shacks at Eskimo Point and Baker Lake, where they live mainly on government relief. Only a few thousand taiga Indians still survive, existing in desperate poverty around dying trading posts in the border forest.

Europeans did not occupy the northern prairies they had despoiled. They hardly even explored them before the day of the airplane. Apart from the Royal Navy's Captain George Back, who in 1834 descended the river bearing his name, and J. B. and J. W. Tyrrell, who between 1892 and 1900 canoed the valleys of the Dubawnt, Kazan and Thelon rivers, and a few such wanderers as James Anderson in 1855, Roderick Macfarlane in 1857, David Hanbury in 1901-2, and John Hornby, who in 1927 left his bones and those of two companions in the Thelon oasis, the northern plains saw few white visitors until the 1920's when white fox became fashionable and reached a peak value. Then traders crowded to the edge of the taiga or pushed a short distance west from the shores of Hudson Bay to compete with one another for the furs trapped by Eskimos and Indians. The traders were followed and sometimes led by a handful of misanthropic white trappers who were collectively known as the Barren Ground Trappers; they chiefly used poison, not traps, and rarely ventured much farther north than the timber. By 1950, coincidentally with the final destruction of the Caribou Eskimos, most of these trappers and all the traders had also vanished from the land. Today an occasional aircraft drones overhead. Now and again a prospecting crew descends on some silent lake. For the rest, nearly half a million square miles of Canada lies vacant.

It need not be abandoned. It *should* not be. Where once millions of caribou prospered, meat-producing mammals could make it possible for man to repopulate the northern prairie. It has been done in Siberia, Lapland, even in Alaska, and it could be done here. Reindeer, herded and semi-domesticated, or muskox and caribou carefully husbanded, could bring new life to this empty land. The world is short of meat. Even now more than half the world's population is starving for protein. *We* may be well fed on steaks and roast beef but we are the exceptions. Deliberately pessimistic reports, some by government employees, have been written to prove that the northern prairies cannot produce any significant amount of meat for human use. These reports are given the lie both by what the tundras *did* produce in the past and by what the tundra regions of Scandinavia and Siberia are producing today. Perhaps an explanation of these gloomy reports can be found in what happened in Alaska. There, the Lomen brothers were instrumental in building up herds of reindeer totalling over two hundred thousand animals. Many of these belonged to Eskimos, and other Eskimos were employed with the Lomens' herds. The intention was to supply meat to the U.S. and the first shipments were duly made and sold at premium prices. Immediately the western cattle and sheep raisers lobbied Washington. In short order, the Lomen interests were expropriated and an embargo was placed on the shipment of reindeer meat. The meat was too competitive. Deprived of efficient management (and of open markets) the great Alaska herds shrank to what could be used locally and scores of Eskimo families who had begun to build new lives based on reindeer herding went back to the old life, or to the dole.

It is not inconceivable that something similar has happened in the Canadian North where reindeer have twice been introduced. The first attempt was made on Baffin Island in the early 1920's when Vilhjalmur Stefansson persuaded the Hudson's Bay Company to lease a huge area in the south of the island and to stock it with reindeer. There were difficulties during the first two years, as was to be expected, but it seems likely that the experiment would have succeeded if the company had persevered. It did not do so chiefly owing to management difficulties, and the preliminary herd soon went wild and disappeared.

The second experiment was far more important. In 1929 the Government of Canada purchased a herd from the Lomen brothers in Alaska and had it driven to the Mackenzie delta – a fantastic trek that took five years to complete. Once arrived in the delta the herd should have increased quickly and new herds ought to have been established from it right across the Canadian North – as was the original plan. But nothing happened.

Spotted Grosbeak; White Crowned Bunting.
— Thomas Pennant's Arctic Zoology, 1792.

The brothers Tyrrell

J. B. and J. W. Tyrrell were the great Canadian explorers of the 19th century and among the greatest ever to go north. Joseph Burr Tyrrell was a government geologist and his brother James was a land surveyor. In their time, the interior of the northern prairie of Keewatin and Mackenzie was virtually unknown, having seen no white man since Samuel Hearne (1769-72). The Tyrrell brothers undertook to change all this: to find out just what Canada possessed in this distant region. During the last decade of the century they made three amazing journeys. In 1893 they went together to the southern headwaters of the unknown Dubawnt River system and in a journey of 3,500 miles, explored it north, then east, to Baker Lake. The following year Joseph paralleled this route farther to the east, by descending the unexplored Kazan River. Then, in 1900, James entered the prairies from Great Slave Lake and explored the Thelon River east to Baker Lake. Between them, the brothers Tyrrell travelled about 10,000 miles by canoe, on foot, and on snowshoes.

From an 18th Century French engraving.

A modern tragedy:

John Hornby, a strange self-exiled English-man, became a legend in the Arctic in his own time. He seemed to seek out hardship for its own sake, and it was rumoured that he could live and travel where an Eskimo would starve. Mostly alone, sometimes with companions of his own stripe, he roamed the tundra from 1904 to 1927. Several times he was given up for lost, but he always returned to the edge of civilization. In 1926 he appeared in the Great Slave country accompanied by a school-boy cousin, 18-year-old Edgar Christian, and a 27-year-old ex-Royal Air Force pilot. With these complete greenhorns, he set out to winter in the very heart of the northern prairies at the Thelon "oasis". Two years later three bodies were found in a decaying little cabin on the Thelon, and in the cook stove was the diary of Edgar Christian. In the simple language of a young boy, this diary tells an almost unbelievably horrible story of the inch-by-inch starvation of Hornby and his two companions.

By the early 1960's the government had decided to liquidate the vestigial Mackenzie herd and would have done so had not private interest volunteered to take it over on a contract basis. In 1966 the herd was under the direction of Sven Johansson, a Scandinavian reindeer breeder who was making heartening progress. Having increased the base herd to 8,000 animals, Johansson plans to bring it up to 30,000 by 1976. A herd this size will produce about 1,000,000 pounds of meat annually, with a cash value of about $300,000. That he is on the right track is shown by events in the Soviet North where a base herd of 2,500,000 animals had been developed by 1966, producing 80,000,000 pounds of meat, large amounts of "chamois" leather and more than a hundred byproducts (including glandular extracts) every year. The industry was also providing steady, high income jobs for about 4,000 native families, which is not far off the entire native population of Canada's far North. Soviet experts with whom I talked in 1966 while visiting some of their reindeer farms told me they expected to raise the base herd to 4,500,000 animals by 1975. Dr. V. N. Andreyev, winner of a Lenin Prize for his reindeer research, has seen our arctic and agrees with top Finnish experts that the reindeer-carrying capacity of the Canadian North is in excess of 2,000,000 animals, even allowing for the presence and increase of native caribou herds. Reindeer meat is a gourmet delicacy in Europe and would find a ready market in southern Canada.

Another possibility is the suggestion that muskoxen be raised like cattle. These animals scarcely need to be herded since they ramble very slowly across the tundra. Their meat is excellent and their wool, finer than cashmere, is even more valuable. Even if we accept the dubious thesis that our cattlemen should be protected against competition from the arctic, and even if we decided to prohibit the shipment of northern meat to southern Canada, we could *still* ship surplus reindeer, caribou and muskox meat overseas via the Canadian Sea route or around Alaska to the Pacific region, to countries that are starved for protein. They would gain — and so would we. In the meantime one of the truly great grazing grounds in the world remains an unused wilderness.

Grazing is by no means the only potential of the tundras. Under the lichens lie many known deposits of minerals which will one day be of extreme value. So far they have largely been ignored because the northern prairie is presumed to be almost inaccessible except by air. In truth it could be opened up with far less difficulty than almost any other part of Northern Canada. All-year roads may not even be needed. The techniques of building winter truck roads of compacted snow, now in use in the Mackenzie basin, are completely applicable to the tundra. In the Soviet arctic such roads have been in use for two generations and the heaviest types of trucks can use them for as much as eight months of the year. As for entry and exit points, both the eastern and the western tundra plains have the Canadian Sea lapping their very shores.

At a time when the vast majority of the Eskimos and Indians of our North have no work to do, no means of livelihood left to them, this immense territory could be made to supply them with an opportunity to recover pride of self, to find freedom from the dole, and to build new lives in a world that is familiar to them. At the same time it would be making Canada a greater nation.

All of the things suggested here could be done if we would expunge from our minds the concept of the northern prairies as a worthless desert. In truth they are full of the gift of life.

THE LIVING NORTH

The North is a living world, intensely alive and inhabited by life in ten thousand forms. Its animals range in size from the greatest beasts of all time – the baleen whales – to microscopic creatures flickering eerily in the green sea-meadows, or crawling through the Lilliputian jungles of moss and lichens on the tundra plains. Casual visitors from the south observing the long, white desolation of winter snows and frozen seas frequently conclude that life is all but absent here. It is not so. Hearts beat and blood pulses under the concealing ice; plants wait and animals breathe slowly under the shifting snows. With spring the waiting ends. The pale skies fill with skeins of crying birds. The foaming seas swirl with seals and swift shadows mark the passage of pods of narwhals. Heavy-bodied char glitter in the shallow waters at river mouths. Gulls wheel about the opening leads in the dissolving ice.

A moving carpet of caribou brings the hot flow of life to the tundra

In May the dispersed herds in the taiga forests flow together and a river of life pours purposefully northward to the plains where the fawns are born. In summer the great throngs dissolve, drifting in little groups, apparently as aimless as the wind. But when the days grow short again the wanderers draw together, coalescing into huge herds in preparation for the journey south. In years gone by a single migrating herd could take ten days to stream past a given point. On the upper Dubawnt River in 1893, explorer J. B. Tyrrell met a herd that he conservatively estimated to contain 200,000 individuals. Such mighty throngs no longer exist, but this picture taken near Bathurst Inlet a few years ago conveys some idea of their magnitude – even though there are fewer than six thousand caribou in sight here.

During the winter most caribou live in small companies deep in the shelter of the spruce forests to the south.

The strange and striking creatures of the North

Narwhal

Arctic fox

Muskox

Moose

Walrus

Lemming

Parry's Ground Squirrel

Arctic wolf

Grizzly bear

Life in the North is characterized by its surprising variety and by its great mobility. Even such specialized arctic beasts as polar bears, pelagic seals, white whales and polar foxes range southward to the verges of our urban world. Beasts that we think of as southern inhabitants reverse the flow and penetrate far into the North: black bears and moose wander far out into the tundra plains; birds arrive in summer from as far afield as Africa. An exception is the muskox who, fearing neither living enemy nor the worst the winter can produce, may die within a few miles of where he was born.

Snowy owl

Rough-legged hawk

Ptarmigan

Tufted Puffin

Plover

Murres

Peregrine falcon

Grey jay

In late summer, the muskeg plains of Southampton Island are mottled, flecked and streaked by thousands of flocks of gleaming white Snow Geese feeding, or sleepily congregating on sunny ridges before their long migration south. About eighty species of birds are known to breed in the Canadian Arctic and, at times, nearly all of them can be seen in one location.

Gentle and ferocious —Northern contrasts

Moving with fluid and bewildering grace, the polar bear fights valiantly when fight he must. Eskimo hunters of a few years ago had to come close to that swaying, lunging head and try conclusions with a spear. In those days, the blood upon the snow was not always the bear's. But now, the hunter stands safe outside the circle of dogs and, with his rifle, makes an easy kill. The great white bear – the king of the Arctic – lives mostly on the sea ice, where he finds the seal, his main food. The cubs are born in snowbank dens at Christmas.

White lichen (*Stereocaulon* sp.)

Arctic crocus (*Pulsatilla ludoviciana*)

White heather (*Cassiope tetragona*)

Arnica (*Arnica alpina*)

Lousewort (*Pedicularis capitata*)

Map lichen (*Rhizocarpon geographian*)

Lichen (*Cladonia coccifera*)

Cotton grass (*Eriophorum scheuchzeri*)

Mountain heath (*Phyllodoce caerulea*)

Northern flora embraces three empires. Southward is the sombre realm of spruce, birch and pine forests under whose protection lesser plants grow high and proud. Beyond lies the northern prairie stretching far up into the arctic islands. Here plants are incredibly abundant, but more circumspect and they grow small and lowly. The third empire is of the waters, both salt and fresh, where rooted sea-weeds wave darkly, and free-floating algae turn tundra ponds into vats of multi-coloured dyes. All three have individual beauty, but the gaiety and brilliance of the diminutive tundra flowers can hardly be matched anywhere in the world.

Purple saxifrage (*Saxifraga oppositifolia*)

Lousewort (*Pedicularis arctica*)

Cress (*Draba bellii*)

Wintergreen (*Pyrola grandiflora*)

Arctic willow (*Salix arctica*)

Rhododendron *(sp. lapponicum)*

Arctic poppy (*Papaver radicatum*)

Arctic wallflower (*Erysimum pallasii*)

Arctic dryas (*Dryas integrifolia*)

ARCTIC OCEAN

NORTH POLE

Franklin's last expedition 1846

Vilhjalmur Stefansson 1914-18

ALEX HEIBERG ISLAND

ELLESMERE ISLAND

BORDEN I.

SVERDRUP ISLANDS

ELLEF RINGNES I.

PRINCE PATRICK I.

PARRY ISLANDS

MAGNETIC POLE

Lancaster Sound

Beaufort Sea

BANKS ISLAND

SOMERSET ISLAND

PRINCE OF WALES ISLAND

AKLAVIK

Amundsen Gulf

VICTORIA ISLAND

Gulf of Boothia

YUKON

Mackenzie R.

COPPERMINE

CAMBRIDGE BAY

KING WILLIAM I.

Queen Maud Gulf

Great Bear Lake

The Empty Islands

7

Canada's northwest coast is not, as some may think, the coast of northern British Columbia – it is the shoreline of the Arctic Ocean running fourteen hundred miles as the raven flies due east from the Alaska-Yukon border to Melville Peninsula. It bounds the Yukon and the districts of Mackenzie and Keewatin to the north, and it forms the southern base for a huge, slanting pyramid of islands thrusting its apex towards the Pole.

The islands are separated from the mainland by a chain of waterways that most Canadians are unaware of: the Beaufort Sea, Amundsen Gulf, Dolphin and Union Strait, Coronation Gulf, Dease Strait, Queen Maude Gulf, Simpson Strait and the Gulf of Boothia. These waters are usually ice free in summer and so provide a natural water road across the top of the continent. The island shores to the north and the mainland shores to the south were once among the most heavily populated areas in the Arctic. The western reaches belonged to the Mackenzie Eskimos, the central area to the Copper Eskimos, and the eastern regions to the Netsilik Eskimos. The latter were lucky people, for they were the last of their race to be wrenched away from the old certainties and thrust into the uncertainties of our world.

Although the Arctic coast was glimpsed by Hearne in 1771 at the mouth of the Coppermine River, and by Mackenzie in 1779 at the mouth of the river named for him, Europeans were slow to follow. Not until the end of the nineteenth century did Yankee whalers poke their noses around Point Barrow in Alaska and begin chasing whales in the Beaufort Sea, using Herschel Island as a base. Not until 1910 did Viljhalmur Stefansson make the first real contact between whites and the Copper Eskimos; and not until the First World War did traders filter eastward as far as the Netsilik country.

But from 1916 onward the interlocked series of waterways along the northwest coast became an avenue of riches for the traders. Since it is a blind avenue (its eastward end is blocked by northward-thrusting Boothia Peninsula) trade goods flowed into it and furs flowed out either around Alaska or up and down the Mackenzie River. In those days the northern shores were still occupied by an almost continuous frieze of small Eskimo settlements. Today the surviving Eskimos are clotted into a few widely separated communities.

Pelly Bay, the farthest east, in the Gulf of Boothia, is a special case since it has no sea communications with the northern shore waterways or with Hudson Bay. Consisting of about two hundred Eskimos, it was for long a

Eskimo sled, constructed of bone, sketched by a member of the Sir John Ross expedition, Baffin Bay, 1818.

theocracy, ruled by a priest of the Oblate order, who was the only white resident; but in the sixties it was invaded by the Department of Northern Affairs who (I am sure with no intended malice) stationed a charming young lady teacher there. Pelly Bay remains the most "primitive" Eskimo community extant, but its younger people have become restive in the new age, and are no longer content to live as anachronisms in a changing world.

Westward from Pelly Bay lies Spence Bay, a non-community arbitrarily sited in a poor hunting area when a Hudson's Bay post at Fort Ross, to the northward, proved too difficult to supply. The majority of the Netsilik people now cluster at Spence where the bleak pattern of the North repeats itself. Free houses, good schools – and no meaningful way to make a living. Westward again on King William Island lies Gjoa Haven. Here the story is much the same, although at least a proportion of the people can still find a limited occupation in seal-hunting and fox-trapping. Gjoa Haven is of some special interest because its clergyman is an Eskimo – one of several who have been ordained in a move by the Anglican Church to replace foreign missionaries by native priests. Southwestward, on the mainland, a rapidly dwindling handful of Eskimo families cling to the old ways at Perry River. Northwest from Perry River, on Victoria Island, is Cambridge Bay – another Frobisher Bay, scaled down a little. Cambridge Bay boasts a DEW Line station and a large and modern airport. It has little else to boast about, for its non-military population consists almost exclusively of government employees and unemployed Eskimos. A multi-million-dollar residential school has been built here for Eskimo children from the whole of the central arctic region. They receive the best education we can offer (much of it meaningless to them, since it is designed for white urbanites). It is just possible, although there is no evidence to demonstrate it as yet, that when they graduate some way will have been found for them to use their new skills to make a decent life for themselves, and to begin the task of reviving what is, in essence, a dying land – for surely a land is dead when men no longer live and work in it, and as a part of it.

West from Cambridge Bay on the mainland shores are the settlements of Bathurst Inlet, where an old-time fur trader has been trying to turn back the clock and persuade the Eskimos to avert their face from the modern world; Coppermine, another burgeoning welfare settlement; and Paulatuk, the home of a handful of Eskimos dispossessed from employment at a DEW Line site. On the island coasts are the small settlements of Holman Island and Sachs Harbour, both of which are doubtless doomed, for they are old-style communities.

The northern shore is a depressing place these days, apparently with little hope and little future. Yet on the islands to the north there *is* hope *and* a future. The paradox is that the bulk of the people live on the moribund coast while the islands to the north are almost empty of mankind.

Texas is big, but the islands of Canada's Arctic Archipelago have a land area three times as large. Texas has oil, but recent estimates suggest that there is several times as much oil under the arctic islands. Texas is cattle country, but most of the larger islands have herds of caribou and muskox. One thing Texas has, however, that the arctic islands lack: people. It has not always been so and may not be so in years to come, but for the moment these are the empty islands of the north.

The archipelago is divided naturally into two parallel tiers separated from each other by the Parry Channel which runs east and west from Lancaster Sound on Baffin Bay to M'Clure Strait on the Beaufort Sea.

The lower tier, bordering the mainland coast, includes Banks, Victoria, King William, Prince of Wales and Somerset islands, as well as Boothia and Melville peninsulas which are peninsulas only in the narrowest technical sense, being joined to the mainland as a nearly severed leg may be joined to the body by no more than a fragment of skin. Baffin Island also belongs to the lower tier.

Victoria and Banks islands, separated from each other only by the narrow Prince of Wales Strait and from the mainland by equally narrow waters, are as big as the entire British Isles. Together with Prince of Wales and King William islands they form an extension of the northern prairies and share the same kind of rolling tundra. Low and monotonous when seen from the air, they too show an amazing richness of detail from the ground.

The straits separating them from the mainland freeze solidly and there is hardly any ice movement during the winter. As a result these several islands are firmly joined to the mainland for as much as eight months of the year. Tremendous herds of caribou used to treat the islands of the lower tier as part of the mainland, migrating northward to them by the hundreds of thousands over the sustaining ice in late spring, and returning southward again early in the winter. The great migratory herds have vanished now, but small remnant herds still remain on the islands all year round, along with perhaps a thousand muskox.

The eastern portion of the lower tier, Somerset Island and Boothia and Melville peninsulas, has a different nature. Much more rugged and bony, the land is cleft with ancient valleys and studded with rounded hills. Nevertheless this region too once harboured good-sized herds of caribou and muskox. Now the muskox have vanished, and only pitiful stragglers of the caribou herds remain. The waters about all of the islands of the lower tier were once very rich in seals, white whales and Greenland whales and would be still rich enough to feed the surviving Eskimos of the coastal regions and to provide the basis of a cash economy based on these renewable resources, if only they were properly managed – which they are not.

In time past Eskimos occupied all these lands, as their numerous abandoned settlement sites still testify. Europeans came early to the islands. In 1819-20 Parry went sailing west down the great channel that bears his name, making a record distance west and almost completing the Northwest Passage. James Clark Ross explored Boothia and Somerset between 1829 and 1833 while with an expedition commanded by his uncle, John Ross, and located the magnetic pole on Boothia. But Boothia has since lost the honour, for the north magnetic pole is a wanderer and in 1966 lay somewhere under the waters of Viscount Melville Sound. Victoria was first seen from the south by Sir John Franklin's overland expedition of 1825-27. East of this island in 1845-48 his grandiose Northwest Passage expedition consisting of two fine ships and 129 officers and men vanished into death and darkness. Only fragmentary details of that tragedy have been recovered by the dozens of search expeditions that penetrated the lower tier from east, west and south, scouring it for traces of the missing voyagers. Apparently the two ships got as far as Victoria Strait between King William and Victoria islands where they were trapped in the ice during the winter of 1846. They remained trapped. Franklin died the next year and his second in command, Crozier, took over. Crozier abandoned the imprisoned ships in 1848 and, dragging heavy oaken boats, began a hopeless trek southward along the coast of King William Island. Singly at first, then in groups the sailors died of scurvy and starvation. A few preternaturally tough

Sir John Ross, a tough and irascible old Scot, was the man who, in 1818, rediscovered Baffin Bay which had not been officially entered (whalers probably had sailed it for some years) since Bylot and Baffin explored it in 1616. Ross also entered the mouth of Lancaster Sound, but took it to be a closed bay. For this error he was savagely criticized in England. Unable to get any more official aid, he turned to private money to finance another expedition in a tiny, steam-paddle yacht called Victory. By sheer determination he forced his fragile vessel well into the Gulf of Boothia (which he named for his distiller sponsor) and there he somehow kept all but three of his original 21 men alive through four arctic winters. Surviving the loss of Victory to the ice, the indomitable Ross led his men north in small boats until they eventually made contact with a whaler near the mouth of Lancaster Sound.

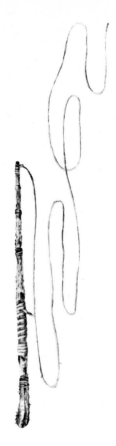

*Bone spear, bone and sinew dog whip.
— Artifacts from the High Arctic.*

individuals got as far as an islet in Chantrey Inlet on the mainland coast where their greening bones were discovered long years afterwards. The story of the Franklin Expedition is one of horror. It need not have been. But men and officers seem to have been so convinced that white men could not live from the land that they stuck to canned and dried foods brought from home while ignoring the bountiful supplies of fresh meat available from sea and land, which could have sustained them as it was then sustaining a large population of Netsilik Eskimos.

A few Netsilik people still hunt on eastern Melville and southern Boothia peninsulas, King William and the south shores of Victoria and Banks islands, but the great hinterland, an area of nearly a hundred thousand square miles of tundra, is, like the tundra of the mainland, devoid of man.

The upper tier is a different land with a different story. It forms the top of the triangle and includes Prince Patrick, Melville, Bathurst, Cornwallis, Cornwall, Amund and Ellef Ringnes, Meighen, Mackenzie King, Borden, Brock, Devon, Axel Heiberg, Ellesmere and a number of smaller islands which together occupy about two hundred thousand square miles of land and water. Axel Heiberg and Ellesmere with eastern Devon belong to the Icy Mountain region. The remainder, apart from those facing south on the Parry Channel were, until recently, among the most inaccessible lands on earth. Some of them, including Mackenzie King, Borden, Meighen and Lougheed, were unknown until Stefansson discovered them between 1914 and 1918.

The Parry group along the Parry Channel consists of high, bold, glacier-rounded highlands, but to the north the islands are part of a vast coastal plain. The extreme north central islands have only recently (in geological time) emerged from the sea, and they are still rising. They tend to be flat, low and formless and most of them are perpetually surrounded by polar ice. They are desert lands, for they have very little rain and snowfall. Plant life is scanty; sedges, mosses and tiny flowering plants struggle against a bitter environment for survival. Nevertheless, all of the islands of the upper tier, except perhaps Meighen, once supported herds of caribou and muskox. Most of them still have small residual herds today. Seals live in the surrounding waters, keeping in touch with the upper world by gnawing breathing holes through the ice cover. Stefansson and his party travelled for months with dog teams, covering thousands of miles through this reputedly uninhabitable world while living almost entirely off the land and sea. Eskimos at one time inhabited many of the islands and in the 1950's several families from farther south were transported to Resolute Bay on Cornwallis to repopulate the Parry Islands. But times have changed and the inoculation did not take. The Eskimos remained clustered at Resolute, a community that bids fair to becoming another Cambridge Bay, another Frobisher Bay.

There are really only three clusters of humanity in the entire region now, and all are recent. Two are the remote weather stations at Mould Bay on Prince Patrick Island and Isachsen on Ellef Ringnes Island. These were established in 1948 by a "joint" U.S.–Canadian effort. The half dozen men at each of these stations do not constitute settlements so much as garrisons of embattled outposts of technology. Resolute is the only settlement deserving of the name. Its prime function is to provide a base for supplying the weather stations and for prospecting the islands of the upper tier. It has a scheduled air service to and from the south and reflects the same type of frenetic activity that briefly characterized life at Frobisher Bay. Resolute's future is almost completely dependent upon exploitation of the non-renewable resources – primarily oil – in the upper islands. Apart from the Eskimos its population is a transient one, although one southern Canadian, the owner and operator of a small charter air service, has moved his family to Resolute and proclaims his determination to make it his home.

Perhaps his optimism is justified. The federal government is in the process of spending many millions of dollars to assist oil exploration companies, all foreign owned, to demonstrate the undoubted existence of large oil fields. In addition a reef of lead-zinc-silver ore, some 250 miles in length, has been discovered running north from Cornwallis Island. This fabulous lode may very well be mined if the Mary's River iron mines on north Baffin Island go into production.

Remote as they may be geographically (Resolute is only six hundred miles farther from Leningrad than it is from Ottawa), the islands of the upper tier are no longer distant in reality. Icebreakers of the Department of Transport make annual supply voyages to Resolute and have steamed west as far as western Melville Island. Aircraft operating on charter out of Resolute are capable of spanning the entire region, and the new technique of equipping very light planes such as Super Cubs with huge low-pressure tires enables them to land almost anywhere a helicopter can put down. Gas and oil exploration permits covering sixty-one million acres of the arctic islands have already been issued and test wells have been sunk in Melville Sound. Northern Canada could use vast quantities of oil to fuel thermo-electric generators. Once the oil begins to flow, it will be possible to export it direct to Europe and Asia as well as south to industrial Canada, so that a continuing market is assured throughout the foreseeable future. The day may come when Resolute will not be the only real foothold of mankind in the islands of the High Archipelago. The day may come when men reclaim these islands which have lain so long abandoned.

Early communications in the Arctic:
(from a book by Sherard Osborn.)

"In 1850 one of the relief expeditions searching for Sir John Franklin wintered at Beechey Island in Lancaster Sound. Sir John Ross aboard Felix had brought passenger pigeons in the hope that they could be used to send messages back to England. The idea was a great joke among the men and I plead guilty to having joined in the laugh when I heard it proposed to despatch the pigeons from Beechey Island to Ayr in Scotland, even though they were to be slung to a balloon for part of the journey. It was tried on the 6th of October, 1850. Two birds freighted with intelligence and with notes from the married men were put in a basket attached to a balloon in such a manner that, after combustion of a certain quantity of fuse, the carrier pigeons would be launched into the air. General opinion was that the birds would be frozen to death. This was mistaken for, in about 120 hours, one of these birds, as verified by the lady to whom it had originally belonged, reached her house in Ayr. This marvellous flight of 3,000 miles is the longest on record."

Arctic freight sled, with huskies. From a sketch by N. Teto in the Canadian Illustrated News, *1871.*

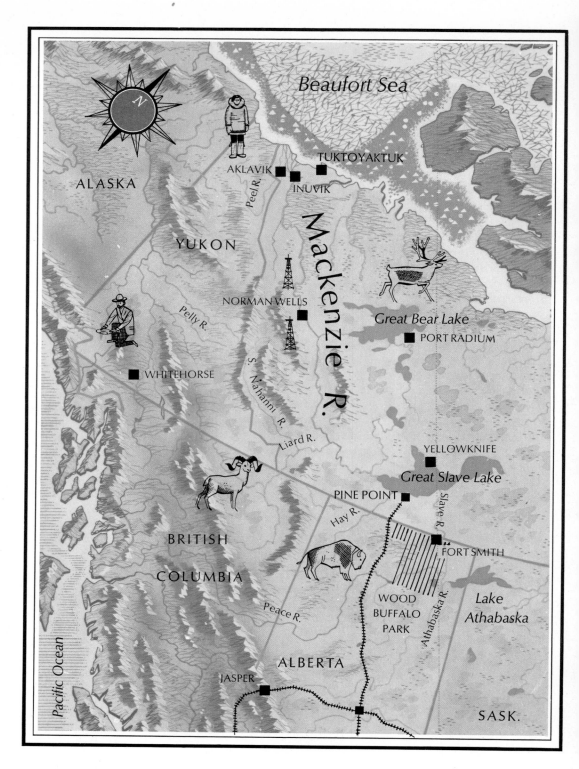

Beaufort Sea

ALASKA

TUKTOYAKTUK

AKLAVIK

INUVIK

Peel R.

YUKON

Mackenzie R.

NORMAN WELLS

Great Bear Lake

PORT RADIUM

Pelly R.

S. Nahanni R.

WHITEHORSE

Liard R.

YELLOWKNIFE

Great Slave Lake

PINE POINT

Slave R.

Hay R.

FORT SMITH

BRITISH

COLUMBIA

WOOD
BUFFALO
PARK

Athabaska R.

Lake
Athabaska

Peace R.

ALBERTA

JASPER

SASK.

Pacific Ocean

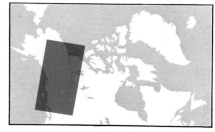

The Great River

8

The two longest and greatest rivers in North America have headwaters in southern Alberta. The most northerly waters of the one become the Milk River and flow southeast into the Missouri, then into the Mississippi and so to the Gulf of Mexico. The most southerly waters of the other rise in the Columbia Ice Field near Jasper, becoming the Athabaska which later becomes the Slave (joined by the Peace) and then becomes the Mackenzie, to flow into the Arctic Ocean at the Beaufort Sea. The mouths of these two rivers are thirty-two hundred miles distant in a direct line, yet their headwaters lie less than three hundred miles apart. One is the Great River of the South, the other is the Great River of the North.

The Great River of the North is a good deal more than the stretch that bears the name Mackenzie. The Mackenzie is only the mighty central flume for a network of many rivers, including the Athabaska, Finlay, Peace, Hay, Liard and the Peel. There are also scores of lesser streams. Among them they drain, northward to the polar ocean, a basin of seven hundred thousand square miles that includes one-third of the Yukon, almost half of British Columbia, more than half of Alberta, one-third of Saskatchewan and most of the District of Mackenzie.

Fierce, foaming rivers from the mountains to the west; placid, muddy rivers from the poplar plains to the south; clear, green waters from the coniferous forests to the east; and brown-stained waters from the tundra to the northeast all draw together into that mighty trough extending northward from the Central Plain of North America. This plain, which begins at the Gulf of Mexico, is in reality the bed of an ancient, shallow ocean that once split North America in two. Its rocks are sedimentary and under them lie immense pools of oil and gas – products of the decay of astronomical numbers of animals and plants. These oil fields have been tapped from Texas north into central Mackenzie and they underlie the valley of the Great River throughout its length. The surface of the valley has been more recently shaped to its present watery purpose by an apron of the great ice sheet which, thrusting westward some ten thousand years ago, encounterd the Mackenzie Mountains. Unable to surmount them, the ice turned north to plow a channel hundreds of miles wide to the Arctic coast. The great sheet, moving west across the Shield, had force enough to gouge a necklace of lakes around the rim of the Shield. Three of these lakes now help feed the Great River. Lake Athabaska, Great Slave and Great Bear lakes form three huge reservoirs although they are diminishing in size – Athabaska having shrunk the

The Indian of the North:

Chief Matonabbee led Samuel Hearne from Churchill across the northern prairie to the mouth of the Coppermine River in 1770. Here is Hearne's own description of this remarkable man.
"He had so much natural good sense and liberality of sentiment that he would not ridicule any particular sect on account of their religious opinion. He held them all in equal esteem, but was determined that as he came into this world, so he would go out of it — without professing any religion at all. Notwithstanding, I have met few Christians who possessed more good qualities, or fewer bad ones. His scrupulous adherence to truth and honesty would have done honour to the most devout Christian, while his benevolence and universal humanity to all the human race could not have been exceeded. He was remarkably fond of Spanish wines, though he never drank to excess; and as he would not take spirits, however good they were, he was always master of himself."

Investigations during 1966-67 seem to prove that Canada has one of the world's greatest oil pools under her arctic lands. When and how it will be developed remains to be seen. It has been suggested that instead of pumping the crude oil out of the country, it should be made the basis for a long-lived petro-chemical industry in the Mackenzie valley. Will we use it for our own national advantage . . . or will we give it away to foreign nations to exploit for their advantage?

most since the departure of the ice sheet. Great Bear and Great Slave have an area of roughly twelve thousand square miles each, making each of them a third again as large as Lake Ontario.

Like its sister to the south the main artery of the Great River of the North is a placid, broad and easy-flowing monster; but unlike its southern sister it flows through no pastoral plains. Its way lies through a forested valley where spruce and birch crowd to the river banks, only giving way to open tundra near the mouth of its vast and complex delta.

There is little monotony on the Great River. In the old days travellers going "down north" on its broad waters began their journeys at the head of rail at Athabaska Landing, north of Edmonton. By canoe or York boat, and later by small stern- or side-wheel steamers, freight and passengers headed down the Athabaska River towards the Arctic coast, passing miles of tar sands made black and sticky by crude oil seeping up from the depths. A hundred and fifty miles from Waterways (a more recent railhead) the river enters Lake Athabaska's western end, not far from the ancient trading post of Fort Chipewyan. Eastward again along the lakeshore lies another kind of settlement: Uranium City, where some of the richest uranium mines in the world poke gaunt head frames into the pale sky. Most of the mines were closed in 1967 and the little town showed the nervous tension that bespoke the uncertainty of its people. Will the town live or die? The need for more bombs or for nuclear-powered generating plants will tell the tale; meanwhile Uranium City wears a brave face and waits.

A dozen miles north of Lake Athabaska the river joins its bigger sister, the Peace, which comes swinging in from the North's most fertile farm lands to the westward. The two unite to become the Slave, crossing the Alberta border into the Northwest Territories at Fort Smith. Here is a new kind of town. Rejuvenated by the Canol project of World War II, it has become a seat of government administration for the new North. Garish rows of suburban bungalows fill geometric clearings in the forest, surrounding shining new faceless buildings filled with stenographers, clerks and administrative officials. Four-engined aircraft land daily at the modern airport and chicly coifed girls straight from Montreal climb into waiting taxis. Only the roar of the white waters over the Rapids of the Drowned (the only important interruption to navigation between Waterways and the Arctic Ocean) reminds the bureaucrats, busy with their papers, that the river at their door is not the Ottawa.

So the river flows, passing lethargically by a huge preserve of rolling parkland, open prairie mingled with birch and poplar bush and with dark muskegs. This is Wood Buffalo Park and here the last important remnants of North America's wood buffalo herds survive. They are driven to slaughtering pens when they become to numerous or, more recently, have been made the targets for the high-powered rifles of wealthy hunters whose Hemingway-type egos need the satisfaction to be found in killing beasts bigger than themselves.

Two hundred miles north of Lake Athabaska the short-lived Slave River empties into Great Slave Lake, along whose shores clusters almost half of the resident (as opposed to transient) white population of the entire Northwest Territories. Here is the most northerly salient southern Canada has established in the High North. It may not be much as yet, but it is a start. On the south shore the town of Hay River has about three thousand white and Indian residents. In 1948 the first highway into the Northwest Territories reached Hay River, and in 1965 it was paralleled by a railroad to Pine Point.

Hay River then became the southern terminus for the Northern Transportation Company, a Crown corporation whose scores of diesel tugs and cargo barges have taken the place of the old side- and stern-wheelers and now transport tens of thousands of tons of freight down the Mackenzie to its mouth for distribution westward along the northern shores as far as Spence Bay. Hay River is also a major fishing port. Fleets of small craft, and several larger vessels sail each summer to harvest whitefish and lake trout. In winter the fishery continues – with nets set through the ice. In 1965 five million pounds of fish were taken from Great Slave and most of this was shipped to southern markets. Thus Hay River is both a transport centre and a fishing town.

Neighbouring Pine Point, some forty miles to the west, is a different sort of place. It was one of the largest mining developments in Canada when it began production in 1966. Its lead-zinc deposits are expected to produce 215,000 tons of concentrates a year to be shipped out on a 437-mile railroad especially built by the Canadian government to link Pine Point with the main lines in the south.

Almost overnight Pine Point became a swinging new northern city. Yet it epitomizes the old attitude towards the North. No smelter has been built to refine the ore and to give permanent jobs to its residents or to the people in nearby communities. Instead the concentrate is being shipped all the way to Trail, B.C., with a minor proportion of it going to Fort Saskatchewan, near Edmonton. This is in sharp contrast to the Soviet system which makes a point of ensuring that raw resources should be processed as fully as possible in the area in which they are found, with the result that really permanent towns take root, rather than the temporary towns that characterize mining in the Canadian North.

On the north shore of the lake, opposite Pine Point, is another mining town, Yellowknife, whose stock-in-trade is gold. Yellowknife began its existence as a mining town in the 1930's. By 1966 time was running out: the ore reserves had largely been depleted. Most of its smaller mines had closed and it was subsisting principally on the employment provided by two remaining mines, Consolidated Mining and Smelting (known as Con), and Giant, which not so long ago was the fourth largest gold mine in Canada. On the eve of the Centennial nobody in Yellowknife liked to talk about it openly, but the writing was already on the wall for both these mines. Nevertheless the four thousand people of the little city remained tenacious in their hopes. They spoke optimistically of new strikes, of a rise in gold prices, or of becoming the administrative capital of the Northwest Territories. Yellowknife residents, many of whom have lived there for two decades, stoutly insisted they were going to stay whether all the mines closed up or not.

The Mackenzie Highway from the south recently reached Yellowknife; so the town has a growing importance as a transportation centre. Five charter airlines fly out of it, and in winter truck convoys of Byers Transport Company pound northward to Great Bear Lake or out to distant Tundra Mine on the edge of the "barrens" to the northeast. These truck convoys travel on roads built of snow which can be used by ordinary tractor trailers (such as we see on our southern superhighways) led by one truck with a snow plow. Byers boasts that it can, and will, make such roads to almost any point north or east of Yellowknife, and there is no reason to doubt the company's ability to do just that.

Hay River, Yellowknife and Pine Point are the brighter lights of the

Newest and most impressive of far northern mining towns, Pine Point looks like a bright symbol for the future. But, in truth, it has little chance of an enduring life. It is simply a shinier model of the old mining towns that existed only as long as there was ore beneath them — ore to be shipped to some far southern point for processing. The concept of developing such a mining town as the seed for an enduring mining-industrial complex that can grow with the years by diversified activity has not yet been accepted in Canada's North.

The use of big and tediously slow crawler tractors to haul heavy goods in and out of remote parts of the Arctic is now old fashioned. In the U.S.S.R., techniques of building winter roads to almost anywhere, over almost any kind of terrain, now permit the high-density use of ordinary heavy highway trucks to move immense amounts of freight at high speed over very long distances.

The whole of Great Bear Lake (175 miles long) has been set aside as a preserve for sport fishermen, and luxurious lodges, served by direct air links with Winnipeg and Edmonton, have sprung into existence. Most of them are owned and patronized by Americans. The lake thaws for only four months a year.

Summer Break-Up:

"Suddenly the murmur of the river flowing beneath its winter ice seemed to swell, to become resonant, then in an instant it was transformed into a heavy-throated roar. The cabin shuddered and the tin plates on the table slid and rattled as if dancing to the erratic rhythm of an earthquake. I caught a terrifying glimpse of an immense cake of ice, at least ten feet thick, rearing out of the river not twenty paces from my door. It stood briefly on end, then toppled forward and as it fell a grey geyser of tormented water flew high above the shifting ice. The river, so long contained, was surging up between the shattered floes. The sound of the breakup moved downstream like the roll of a giant drum. As it passed, a violent cacophony came into being as the great cakes shattered and moved ponderously down toward the still frozen lake. The air above the battleground was filled with a fine dust of ice crystals. Floes the size of buildings were ground out of existence in mere moments to be instantly replaced by others which drove the stubborn bay ice slowly backward."

Great Slave Lake area. There are darker shadows in between. There is the town of Fort Rae, an Indian community now reached by road from Yellowknife where several hundred people are kept alive primarily by welfare payments. These are people we have deemed expendable. Now that the fur trade can no longer give them a livelihood they have no one to turn to except the welfare office. Unsuited by training and history to move suddenly into the tight discipline of an eight-to-five job, they are rejected as potential manpower by most mine owners. The people at Rae are not alone. From Great Slave Lake to the mouth of the Mackenzie the sorry story is much the same. The Indians and Métis who were useful to us when there was money to be made from furs are no longer of use. Today the value of ranch furs far outweighs the value of wild furs. As late as 1960 all the wild furs trapped in the Canadian North returned less than an average one hundred dollars a head to the native peoples. The fur trade is effectively finished, as even the Hudson's Bay Company tacitly admits by the conversion of most of its northern trading posts into mundane general stores.

Leaving Great Slave Lake the river swings westward until it brings up hard against the massive wall of the Mackenzie Mountains where it turns north and, for two hundred miles, runs between ranges that tower high on either bank. At the northern end of this trough the Mackenzie is joined by Great Bear River. Great Bear Lake, which lies about eighty miles to the westward, is one of the largest lakes in the world. Part of it lies north of the Arctic Circle and all of it is deathly cold – only a few degrees above freezing. Yet it is by no means sterile. In the past few years it has become a mecca for wealthy sports fishermen and there are several lodges along its shores where, for as little as nine hundred dollars a week, you can live in luxury and catch lake trout weighing forty pounds and more. In 1966 all but one of these lodges were owned by Americans. Commercial fishing is not allowed on Great Bear Lake, the whole lake having been set aside as a sportsman's preserve.

On the eastern side of the lake lies the now silent town of Port Radium where Gilbert LaBine found pitchblende back in 1930 and started Canada's first radium mines. During World War II the government took over the property because the ore was rich in a substance that had suddenly become all-important – uranium. It is believed to have been uranium from this mine that was used in the manufacture of the Hiroshima bomb. Now the mine is closed.

All the old fur trade settlements between Great Slave and Great Bear lakes depend to a large extent on government largesse. Fort Resolution, Fort Providence, Fort Simpson, Wrigley, Fort Norman and Fort Franklin – all are semi-ghost towns peopled by living ghosts – the Indians of the Great River. But a little farther down stream there is a variation on the theme. At Norman Wells (owned by Imperial Oil, a subsidiary of Standard Oil of New Jersey) scores of oil wells stand capped and quiescent. A few are working and there is just enough activity, enough shining modern equipment, to make a fierce contrast with the other river settlements – yet Norman Wells is only a semblance of what it could become. Under it lies an immense pool of oil first discovered in 1920. The field boomed during World War II when, at fabulous expense, the Canol Pipeline and Highway were built westward across the Mackenzie Mountains, through the Yukon to Whitehorse, then carried northwest to Alaska. The oil from Norman was intended to fuel the Allied war machines in the north Pacific, but shortly after the oil began to flow across the mountains the war ended. The oil *could* have kept on flowing, for Alaska needed it and so did the Yukon. A short extension of the line could have brought the oil to tide-water on the Lynn Canal and so made it available to British Columbia. But the line had never worked well and the flow was cut off. The Canol pipe was sold to scrap dealers and the Canol road allowed to fall into decay.

As an ironic commentary on the way we manipulate our raw resources, oil has once again begun to glitter like gold in the Far North. Millions are now being spent in the search for new fields, *far to the north of the capped wells at Norman*. It is known that oil-producing formations extend north along the valley of the Great River towards the Arctic coast on a front 250 miles wide! It is estimated that the potential reserves of this formation total the astronomical sum of twenty-one million barrels – about seven times the reserves of all of Western Canada. These colossal pools will someday be tapped, but the chances are that the crude oil will be pumped through pipelines to the south for refining and the new fields will bring only a handful of new people into the northern lands. Today Norman Wells itself produces only a trickle of oil and distillate products – just enough to meet the needs of the Mackenzie River district and of the communities of the northeast Arctic coast.

Beyond Norman lie other crumbling citadels – Fort Good Hope, Arctic Red River and, off to the west on the Peel River, Fort McPherson. Then the Great River scents the distant sea and splays out into the delta. This is a fabulous world: more than fifteen hundred square miles of intricate braided channels, innumerable ponds, sloughs and muskeg swamps – the whole alive with muskrats. Not so long ago it was one of the most productive trapping areas in the world. In 1950 white, Indian and Eskimo trappers took three hundred thousand muskrat pelts and sold them at an average of two dollars each. Now the price of rats is so low that it is hardly worth trapping them. And the town that was built on muskrat fur – Aklavik, in the middle of the delta – has become just another village with little reason to exist.

By rights Aklavik should be stone dead. In 1954 the government undertook to build a new city near the mouth of the Mackenzie. After one look at the muddy swamp that cradles Aklavik – entirely unsuitable for large buildings or air strips – it decided to build the model town on the glacial hill on the eastern side of the delta. It was to be called Inuvik – Place of the People (meaning of the Eskimos and Indians).

Inuvik is now the showplace of the north as far as official visitors are concerned. At a cost of many millions a complex of residential schools (duplicate facilities for Catholics and Protestants), hospital, administrative buildings, hotel, research centre, business block, apartments and elegant homes were erected. All were linked to one another by a multi-branched umbilicus known to the planners as a Utilidor; but to the Indians and Eskimos as the "tin lizard". The Utilidor is an ugly self-heating box-like structure covered with corrugated steel that brings running water and steam heat to every building of the new complex and carries off the sewage. Inuvik was a triumph of inventiveness; but the planners deliberately omitted one thing. They built fine houses (with Utilidor) for the innumerable government officials, nurses, teachers, scientists, sociologists, police, preachers, and other whites who were deemed indispensable, but they arranged nothing for the Indians and Eskimos. Inuvik was designed purely as a white administrative centre.

The people of Aklavik were given to understand that no further money would be spent on their community and that they must move to Inuvik;

Arctic Char:

This most succulent of northern fishes has a circum-polar range and has been the pièce de résistance at arctic dinners for centuries. According to some connoisseurs, it is tastier than Atlantic salmon, and it is becoming a gourmet dish in southern Canada. One confirmed booster of the North says: "if we can't turn southerners into Arcticphiles through the use of reason, then we'll do it through their stomachs."

Wood Buffalo:

Most of the great land mammals of the North are threatened with extinction. One that almost disappeared was the wood buffalo, close cousin to the vanished buffalo of the American prairies. Given protection at the last moment, the shaggy wood buffalo is now holding its own within the confines of a huge preserve of 17,300 square miles, established in 1922 mostly in northern Alberta.

and, even though it was a long way from the best hunting grounds, most of them did as they were told. They had to live outside the "Utilidor Palace", so they built their own homes in what is now known, though not by officialdom, as West Inuvik, one of Canada's newest slums. Without sanitation or water it was a hard place to live in. To complicate matters it soon developed that the fine new town had little employment for the natives, except as janitors, servants and maintenance men for Inuvik East.

When all this became clear a strange thing began to happen. Eskimos and Indians, instead of being grateful for the new city, began to leave it. Many of them drifted back to Aklavik and there they dug in their heels and stayed. In 1966 a reluctant government accepted the inevitable and agreed that Aklavik should be allowed to go on living. What Aklavik's ultimate fate may be remains anyone's guess.

Far out on the east side of the delta there is one other settlement: Tuktoyaktuk, often called Tuktuk or simply Tuk. It is the down-river terminus of the Northern Transportation Company and the trans-shipment point for the sea-lift along the coast to the westward. Of the 424 Eskimos who formed the body of the settlement in 1966, two were employed at the nearby DEW Line station, fifteen to twenty worked on the boats in summer, six worked for the Department of Northern Development and four or five for the R.C.M.P. and the Hudson's Bay Company. The rest got along as best they could. A few still manage to trap enough furs to make a miserable existence, but most must accept assistance from the government. Yet by northern standards, Tuk is a relatively prosperous place. Not only does it have the Northern Transportation Company, a DEW Line site, and administrative employment, it is also a base from which wealthy tourists are taken fishing for Arctic char and hunting for white whale along the Arctic coast. In addition it possesses a fur-garment manufacturing co-operative which has been very successful in the past.

Tuk has one special claim to fame – it is the home of pingos. These are weird pimples rising up to two hundred feet from the dead flat, water-logged delta plain. They are actually hills of clear blue ice covered with tundra vegetation, which have erupted as the result of frost action on the frozen delta silt. These pingos have a thin covering of moss and turf that insulates them from the summer sun. One of them has been taken over by the members of the Tuk Chamber of Commerce who are tunnelling into it intent on building the first curling rink in the world inside a pingo.

The country of the Great River is taiga country, and the taiga is a world of its own. Those who fly over its apparently endless reaches of dark coniferous forest are sometimes repelled by its sombre singularity; but those who travel through it, by canoe in summer or by dog team in winter, often come to love it with great intensity: there are some white men who, having lived in it for a few years, are never again able to abandon it. As for the Athapascan Indians whose land it truly is, they wish for nothing better even though it is no longer able to sustain them.

The forests of the taiga are mainly composed of black spruce and jack pine with, here and there, stands of sinuous white birch. In the muskeg regions the trees crowd close, but towards the northern limits of the domain of trees there are regions mostly of spruce, each tree set in a floor of thick green and yellow reindeer lichens that are as soft underfoot as any deep-pile carpet. These areas are parklands where a man can walk for hours, or days, as freely as he can walk in a city park. They were the favourite winter haunts of the caribou that migrated south off the tundras in October or November. Here, and to the south, moose intermingled with the caribou but lived their own secluded lives. Fur-bearers are still abundant, though most are no longer of much commercial value: beaver, martin, wolf, weasel, wolverine, and many others. The snowshoe hare feeds the carnivores – and sometimes man, when times grow very lean. The rivers and lakes provide lake trout, whitefish and often Arctic char. But the caribou was the real lifeblood of the taiga and without it the taiga becomes a land of starvation for the people of the deer.

There is little sawmill timber in the taiga. Instead there is an almost limitless supply of pulpwood. The taiga of the Canadian North could supply the entire world's pulpwood needs throughout the foreseeable future if we chose to use it properly. We have not touched this resource as yet, but there is no reason why we should not do so. Limitless raw materials and cheap hydro-electric power ought to have made the pulp forests of the Far North a mainstay of our economy – as the taiga timber has become a mainstay in the northern regions of the U.S.S.R., where it not only gives wealth to the nation, but supplies tens of thousands of permanent jobs for the native peoples and for immigrants from farther south. Someday perhaps. . . .

The Great River and its broad valley is the most populous part of the Northwest Territories. It has the best climate. It is replete with natural resources: minerals, oil, forests, water power, fish and mammals. It is even possible to farm on a small scale at many places along its great length. Served by both highway and railroad as far as Great Slave Lake, by river transportation to its mouth and by a scheduled airline service all the way north to Inuvik, it surely should be attracting new residents in quantity. It is doing nothing of the kind. Despite isolation pay and all sorts of fringe benefits, the mines at Yellowknife have a chronic labour problem that is getting worse – they simply cannot get enough southern Canadians to come north to work even for a short time, let alone to live. Pine Point is experiencing the same difficulties. Surely this is an ominous intimation of the shape of things to come, for if southern Canadians will not venture north even to these relatively domesticated regions where they can live secure within a simulacrum of their own southern towns, what will they do with the vast bulk of the North – the vast bulk of their own country?

The waters of the Great River flow steadily northward. Will we eventually follow after? Time will tell.

The influence of the Hudson's Bay Company on the country as a whole has been tremendous. Incorporated in 1670, it owned and governed about one-and-a-half million square miles of Canada for two hundred years. It founded the cities of Winnipeg, Victoria, Edmonton and others. H.B.C. employees like Samuel Hearne, Dr. John Rae, Thomas Simpson and Warren Dease explored vast tracts of the tundra and arctic coasts. Most of northern B.C. and the Yukon was first explored by such men as Samuel Black, John Bell and Robert Campbell. In its natural pursuit of profits it, as much as any single agency, brought the northern Indians and the Eskimos into contact with the white man's world.

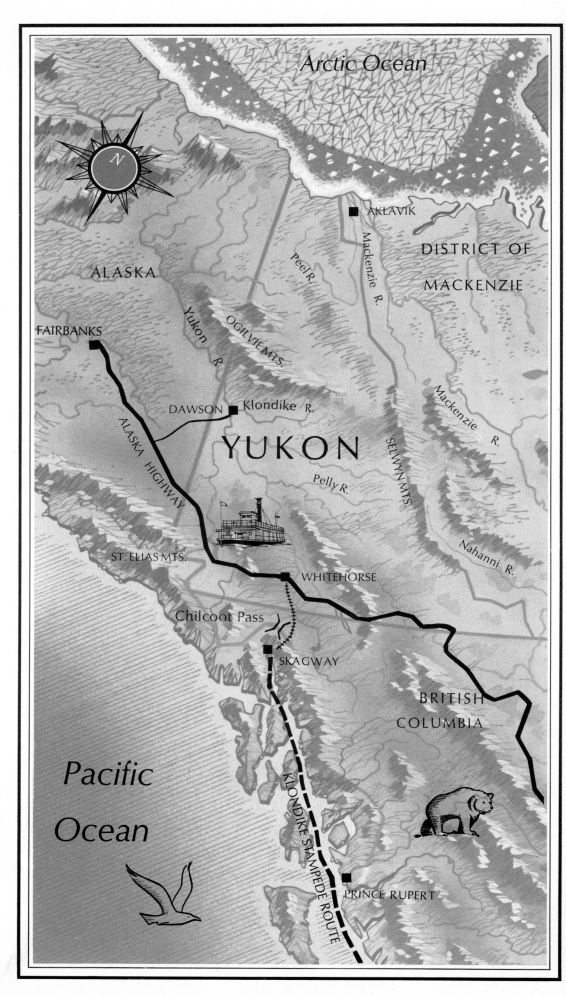

Arctic Ocean

AKLAVIK

DISTRICT OF MACKENZIE

ALASKA

Peel R.

Mackenzie R.

FAIRBANKS

Yukon R.

OGILVIE MTS.

DAWSON Klondike R.

YUKON

Mackenzie R.

ALASKA HIGHWAY

Pelly R.

SELWYN MTS.

St. ELIAS MTS.

Nahanni R.

WHITEHORSE

Chilcoot Pass

SKAGWAY

BRITISH COLUMBIA

Pacific

Ocean

KLONDIKE STAMPEDE ROUTE

PRINCE RUPERT

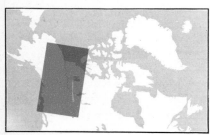

The Western Highlands 9

Westward from the valley of the Great River lies a part of the North that is a very special country. Although it is smaller and less formidable than Tibet (and boasts no lamas) the two regions have their similarities. The Western Highlands consist of an up-thrust, roughly triangular block of ancient, folded mountains amounting to a quarter of a million square miles of peaks, plateaus, glaciers, canyons, tundra plains and broad mountain-guarded river valleys. Four-fifths of this massive eruption of the earth's surface goes to make up the Yukon Territory. The remainder forms a bulbous projection pushing eastward into the District of Mackenzie. Although it is a northward extension of the same parent structure as the Rockies, it is not a part of them, for the great east-west valley of the Liard divides the two.

On its eastern verges the Western Highlands rise in a series of gigantic steps beginning with the Canyon Ranges whose feet stand almost in the waters of the Mackenzie River. The canyons are deeply slashed by harshly sculptured valleys savagely cut by roaring rivers like the Mountain, Keele, Twitya, Redstone and, most dramatic of all, the South Nahanni. The Nahanni, with its limestone pinnacles, sunless clefts, fantastic cliffs, and appalling rapids, has exercised a baleful influence on all white men who have seen it. No other region in Canada has accumulated so many dark legends: semi-human monsters who behead intruders; madness that overwhelms strangers; lost gold mines that offer only death to those who stumble on them; hot-spring valleys filled with tropical vegetation and tropical beasts. The legends are only legends, but the reality is impressive enough. Rising below peaks nine thousand feet high, the Nahanni rages southeastward to the Liard, thundering over Virginia Falls in a drop of 316 feet.

Beyond the Canyon Ranges loom the Backbone Ranges, dominated in their turn by the magnificent, glacier-encrusted Selwyn Mountains whose peaks reach to more than ten thousand feet. The Selwyns form the top of the wall – to the west lie the Highlands: the Yukon Plateau, Peel Plateau and Porcupine Plain, divided from one another and bisected and traversed by mountain massifs.

The Yukon Plateau is by far the largest. It is walled off from its two northern neighbours by the brooding Ogilvie Mountains; cut off from the Pacific Ocean by the St. Elias Mountains whose mighty peaks, lancing up through a vast glacier complex, reach eighteen thousand feet in Canada

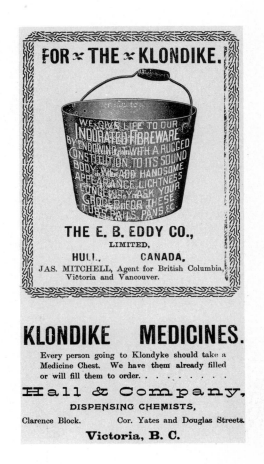

(and twenty-four thousand feet in nearby Alaska) and from British Columbia to the south by the northern buttresses of the Cassiar and Coastal Ranges.

The Peel Plateau and Porcupine Plain between them occupy the Highlands north of the Ogilvie Mountains and are themselves walled in on the east by the Richardson Mountains, and on the north (almost at the Arctic coast) by the British Mountains. The Porcupine and Yukon plateaus extend westward to occupy much of central Alaska; but this is alien soil. Here is the one place where our North borders directly on a foreign country.

Each of the three highland plateaus is drained by a river bearing its name. The Peel River is an oddity, for it flows eastward through a gap between the Richardson and Selwyn mountains to join the Mackenzie. The Porcupine, lying farthest north, flows westward into Alaska where it eventually becomes part of the mightiest of the three rivers – the Yukon. The Yukon is North America's third longest river. Although some of its headwaters rise in British Columbia within fifteen miles of tide-water on the Pacific Ocean, it empties into Alaska's Norton Sound at the Bering Sea after running a course of more than twenty-two hundred miles! Except for its upper reaches it is navigable to shallow-draft vessels, and much of the system offers superb canoe routes. It is an ancient river, much older than the St. Lawrence or the Mackenzie, for it alone of all the major rivers of the North was not obliterated, reshaped or redirected during the last great glaciations. The titanic ice sheet that covered most of Canada and spread far south into the United States stopped short about halfway across the Western Highlands leaving most of the Yukon and Porcupine basins untouched. To the south, the ice blanketed British Columbia and part of the Yukon Territory. The St. Elias glaciers remain as shrunken relics of its one-time presence. To the north an ice-free "oasis" evaded the ice age. Here relict populations of forgotten beasts, including the mammoth and the mastodon, survived long after the majority of their species had been overwhelmed by time, and their bones are still being unearthed by prospectors and gold dredges.

Because of its antiquity the Yukon River has had ample time to wear down the ancient barriers that must once have obstructed its passage with innumerable falls and rapids. It was a natural and easy human highway as much as thirty thousand years ago. Some of the earliest immigrants to North America from Asia ascended the broad waterway of the Yukon into and through the maze of interior mountains. From the headwaters of the Porcupine they crossed McDougall Pass, the lowest elevation (1,000 feet) in the whole Rocky Mountain Range, to the Peel and so emerged into the valley of the Mackenzie. From the Pelly they crossed to the Liard and down it to enter the Mackenzie drainage basin, which they ascended to the forests of what is now northern Alberta. From the Teslin they emerged on the Pacific coast well inside the protective corridor of islands that leads south to Vancouver and beyond.

In our age men have gone the other way. Although Hudson's Bay Company explorers ascended the Liard early in the nineteenth century and explored part of the Yukon, it was not until late in 1883 that a white man, Lieutenant Frederick Schwatka of the U.S. Army, starting at the headwaters of the Yukon, followed the entire stream down to its distant mouth. At the very end of the century uncounted thousands of gold-seekers poured into the headwaters of the Yukon from the Pacific side; others came down the Mackenzie to the Peel and journeyed up it to cross to the Yukon; others ascended the Liard to cross into the Pelly and the Teslin.

The ice sheet that rasped out the raw face of the rest of the Canadian

Lieut. Frederick Schwatka at 34 became the first man to trace the whole 2,000 miles of the Yukon River. Earlier, he searched for Franklin in the Arctic. Below: his King William I. camp.

North spared not only most of the rivers of the Western Highlands, but also the lands, so that the face of the country went largely unscathed. It is an incredibly ancient face, aged by the almost imperceptibly slow processes of water and wind erosion. An aura of unimaginable antiquity lies over the inner plateaus where once-mighty mountains of a million or more years ago have been weathered into elusive, amorphous shapes whose highest places – and some are still six thousand feet high – are no longer shaggy peaks but gently rounded domes. In most parts of the North the ice sheet swept away the soils and sediments accumulated through the millennia, leaving the naked rock exposed. But on the plateaus of the Western Highlands the silts and sediments lie so thick that one can fly many hundreds of miles over them and see no rock, not even on the highest hills.

Because they were never denuded of their soils the plateaus are very fertile. Between two hundred and fifty thousand and five hundred thousand acres of arable land exist in the Yukon alone although only a few thousand acres have so far been put to agricultural use. Forests of commercial timber extend much farther north here than anywhere else in Canada. Apart from alpine tundra high on mountain slopes, and the drowned muskegs of the Porcupine Plains far to the north, tree life in one form or another occupies most of the Western Highlands. Animal life is spectacularly abundant and varied. Along with caribou and moose, the Western Highlands harbour many animals unique in the Canadian North: Dall sheep, mountain goats, cougars and tiny rabbit-like pikas are some of these. Grizzly, black and brown bears can be embarrassingly abundant. Great runs of salmon come thousands of miles from the Pacific up the main stream of the Yukon and into most of its main tributaries.

Although the Western Highlands owe the wealth of their fauna and flora to their escape from the ice, that escape left man a legacy he values even more – rich lodes of placer gold.

Placer gold accumulates as erosion gradually eats away the old rocks and the gold-bearing quartz is ground down in the natural rolling-mills of streams and rivers. In grains ranging from microscopic flecks to fair-sized nuggets the free gold sinks to the stream bottoms, eventually working its way right down to bedrock because of its relatively great weight. Over the eons these deposits were often covered as rivers shifted their beds. Sometimes new streams uncovered old deposits. But if an ice sheet had moved across such an area, the protecting upper layers of sand and gravel would have been stripped away and the placer gold with them. It was the presence of this untouched placer gold in the Yukon that brought about one of the paradoxes in the story of the Canadian North.

In 1967, when Canada was only just beginning to think about bringing the North into the national fold and making it an integral part of our country, it was strange to remember that some sixty-eight years earlier a portion of the Far North had a "white population" as large as that of the region that was later to become the Prairie Provinces, and boasted a city larger than any west of Winnipeg. In 1900 a section of the North, two hundred thousand square miles in extent, was on the verge of becoming a full-fledged province.

At the end of the nineteenth century the Yukon filled the world's eye, and was better known internationally than all the rest of Canada put together. Its freakish rise to prominence began in August, 1896, when squaw-man George Carmack and his Indian companions "Skookum" Jim and "Tagish" Charlie found gold in the bed of Bonanza Creek near the

present site of Dawson. When news of the strike reached the outside world the greatest gold rush in history began. Without benefit of radio, television or jet aircraft, word spread round the world with astounding speed. English peers, Transylvanian peasants, southern planters, Finnish reindeer herdsmen, Australian diggers, Maori tribesmen – men and women from at least fifty nations began to move like lemmings to one of the most remote corners of the known world. Nobody can now say how many actually reached the Yukon, but a figure of eighty thousand is probably not far off the mark.

This massive wave of immigrants into the remote northwest caught Canada off balance. Although the Yukon had been defined as a "provisional" district in the Northwest Territories in 1895, there was nothing in the area to represent government and during the first months of the great Klondike rush anarchy ruled to such an extent that the United States contemplated moving into the vacuum "to protect its own nationals". If the U.S.A. *had* moved in we can be reasonably sure she would never have moved out again. But whatever plans she may have had were scotched when Ottawa rushed small detachments of the military and the North West Mounted Police into the Yukon to plant the flag.

Chaos was reduced to a semblance of order and in 1897 the Yukon became a judicial district. But by the next year the population had grown so huge that a bewildered Parliament passed the Yukon Territory Act and gave the new country of the North the beginnings of real government – one that, by 1908, was to have consisted of a fully elected council as a penultimate step to giving the Yukon provincial status. Yukoners dreamed great dreams in those days. Never before or since had so many men been so willing to make the Canadian North their permanent abode.

Unhappily the final step was never taken and the great dreams died. By 1905 the days of the golden phenomenon in the North were already passing. Although more than one hundred million dollars in gold had by then been taken from the creek bottoms in the Klondike-Dawson region by small operators, their days were done. Big international interests such as Guggenheim began systematically to buy up the claims. Placer mining became mechanized and the small miners were rapidly squeezed out – the big dredges implacably eating their way through private claims. Almost as rapidly as it had been populated, the Yukon was depopulated. Dawson City, which had twenty-five thousand people in 1898 (by far the largest town we have *ever* had in the North) began to shrink at an appalling rate, while nearby towns such as Grand Forks, Gold Bottom, Paris, Caribou and Two Below not only shrank, but vanished utterly.

By 1910 nothing really remained of the great Yukon dream except indelible memories, a few intractably individualistic prospectors, and the thunderous clankings of huge gold dredges methodically stripping the creek bottoms for the benefit of financiers and investors, most of whom did not live in Canada at all. Yukon Consolidated, the greatest of the big companies, was largely owned by South African interests.

The Yukon offered us our first great chance to colonize the North and make it a part of the nation. We lost the chance as we have lost every similar chance since those days. Need we have done so? Today, although the big companies have worked and reworked most of the placer gravel several times and have now abandoned the creeks (the last big dredge ceased working in 1966), a few individuals are still placer mining isolated pockets that the dredges could not reach. I visited one of these independent operations in 1966. It was owned by a man and his wife employing two or

Klondike Memories

In three summer trailer-trips to the Yukon, Canadian painter Alan Collier sketched the streets and sights of Dawson City, and the nearby moldering relics of Canada's greatest gold rush. Dawson once boasted 25,000 citizens; at last census it had dwindled to 846 souls. The last dredge has clanked into silence now and only a few rugged individuals still pan the Yukon tributaries which, at the turn of the century, poured millions in the pokes of a very few lucky sourdoughs.

Bravely alone now, a house still lives.

Notorious saloons have been restored.

Versemaker Robert W. Service clerked in this tin-clad Dawson bank.

Middle: Arizona Charlie's original Palace Grand.

Klondike, *most famed of river steamers, now delights Yukon tourists.*

Once-palatial home still houses a Dawson family.

Like a mechanical behemoth, this dredge lies abandoned in Bonanza Creek, near Dawson. The artist's son climbed all over it.

three helpers. In one recent year this claim yielded more than thirty thousand dollars' worth of gold, making a comfortable living for its owners and paying reasonably good wages to the employees.

Placer mining is one of the very few types of mining that do not require huge amounts of capital and equipment. Individuals can make a continuing living at it. The quarter of a billion dollars in gold taken out of the placer deposits – and out of the country – by the dredging operations of the big companies could have provided a sustaining livelihood for many people in the Klondike region for generations. A mining expert in Dawson City, a forty-year resident, estimated that if the Klondike creeks had remained small holdings (taking into account the effects of new and better methods of placer mining developed through the years) they would still be providing a good income for as many as five thousand resident miners and their families. At the time he told me this Dawson had a population of eight hundred and was fading fast. The last dredge was already grinding to a halt and the Yukon Consolidated Gold Corporation had announced that it was closing down all operations in the area. The *coup de grâce* had been administered to Canada's first city of the North.

Today the Yukon is not much more than a name to most Canadians. The Klondike legend has overmastered the reality to such an extent that the Western Highlands have receded into a kind of limbo. It is not total. The Yukon is not really dead. In fact the southern town of Whitehorse, with a population of about five thousand, is probably our largest northern "city". But the prosperity of Whitehorse is not representative of the Yukon as a whole. The northern portion of the Western Highlands has receded into the mists of memory. Within a few years Dawson will be a ghost town. The mighty Yukon River, which once knew as many as sixty-five big stern-wheelers plying its waters in a single season, has lost some of its might and majesty, and is silent and abandoned save for a handful of diesel-driven boats. The native peoples have been reduced to the state of their brothers in the valley of the Mackenzie. There are only about two thousand Indians left in all of the Yukon, and the majority of these have no work, no hope, no future. North of Dawson there is only *one* remaining Indian settlement – Old Crow on the Porcupine, where two hundred and forty Loucheux Indians scrape

The accidents of fate have made White-horse one of the very few viable towns in the Canadian North. Because the Alaska Highway and the Yukon's only railroad both pass through it, it has become a transportation and tourist centre of some importance. But the vast interior of the Western Highlands must develop first before Whitehorse can become the full-fledged city it dreams of being.

out a bare existence, surviving largely on government handouts.

The Yukon lives today only in its southwest corner, and credit for the existence of this slight flame does not belong to us. It is due to the fact that early in World War II the United States required an overland link with Alaska, and undertook the construction of the Alaska Highway, which had to cross Canadian soil. The building of the Alaska Highway made Whitehorse an important transportation centre. The highway itself has given the Yukon one of its few sustaining industries: tourism. It also, of course, made it easier for mining promoters to reach new properties and some new, or at least recent, mines have come into production: notably United Keno's silver, lead and zinc mines at Mayo, and a hard-rock gold mine just west of Carmack. But in 1967 these were the only producing mines in the Yukon – in a region where base-metal finds alone have been recorded by the score.

The Yukon still has dreams of a sort. Out on the muskegs of the Porcupine Plain drilling rigs are probing for oil. Undoubtedly the oil is there but whether it will be developed and, if so, whether it will benefit the Yukon or simply outside companies remains to be seen. A fabulously rich iron ore deposit has been found in the Selwyns, but the cost of transporting it "outside" is prohibitive and will remain so for a long time. But still, the Yukon dreams. Visions of fantastic strikes haunt the place, and "tomorrow" is the watchword. Whether "tomorrow" will only be a continuation of today – a continuation of the process of despoilment for quick returns – or development with a view to making it possible for many Canadians to live good lives in the magnificent lands of the Western Highlands: this is the question Canada must answer.

This is a question the answer to which concerns not the Yukon alone, but the whole of that vast northern world which truly is an unknown land. Through many generations, Canadians have been singing of the nation in the north that stretches "from east to western sea". Surely the time has come for us to realize – and to act upon the realization – that the True North stretches to yet *another* sea; and that if we are to remain either strong or free, we must at long last take full and real possession of the neglected and rejected taiga, tundra and polar world, making it a veritable part of our nation and becoming part of it ourselves.

For half a century after the Klondike Stampede, the rattle and roar of the great gold dredges echoed through the valleys of the Yukon placer belt. Now the last of them lies abandoned, rotting in its own vast pile of tailings. The old familiar story comes to its inevitable end: Once the minerals are exploited, the mines close and the local settlements wither and die, as Dawson City itself is withering and dying on the banks of the Yukon River.

A. Y. Jackson

A PAINTER'S NORTH

In the sixty years of his love affair with the unique look of Canada, Alex Jackson has earned a sourdough's knowledge of the North (*above:* at 84, at work on Carol Mountain in Labrador) and, on three occasions, he has toted his splattered sketchbox into the high Arctic. In 1925, five years after Jackson and a bunch of rebellious young Canadian painters formed the Group of Seven, he wangled a trip in a government ship to Bache Peninsula, Ellesmere Island. Sunday-painter (and co-discoverer of insulin) Dr. Frederick Banting

squeezed into the cabin with him. At Canada's most northerly post, they just missed spending the winter as the sea ice threatened to lock the ship in the Kane Basin. Again with Banting, Jackson went to Great Slave Lake in 1928 and, this time, so many mosquitoes got into Jackson's paint that he could make only pencil drawings. He returned to Ellesmere with Lawren Harris in 1930 and they noted the incredible blue of old ice floes and the silvery slopes along Hudson Strait. They saw hundreds of gulls roosting.on, and devouring, a dead whale. "An edible island," Jackson said, "must be a gull's idea of paradise." When an Alpine Club group flew to Pangnirtung, Baffin Island, in 1964, the tireless Jackson went along. He asks: "Is all this vast and lovely country to be turned over to the Kodachrome operators?" Today, honoured with a C.M.G., a Canada Council Medal, equipped with a memory as sharp as a raven's eye and a smile like the swift stroke of summer on the tundra, Jackson seldom thinks of the past. He's got a heap of painting to do.

"Near the September Mountains . . . an
exciting country, like a rich tapestry—
with big boulders strewn about everywhere."

While he sketched this scene north-east of Great Bear Lake,
Jackson's group had a plan if attacked by a Barrens Land
grizzly: one man would drench the bear with the gasoline
they used to clean their brushes, another would strike a
match and the third member would film what transpired.

"Off 'Greenland's Icy Mountains,' the sea
was full of the wrecks of old ice floes worn
into all kinds of fantastic forms."

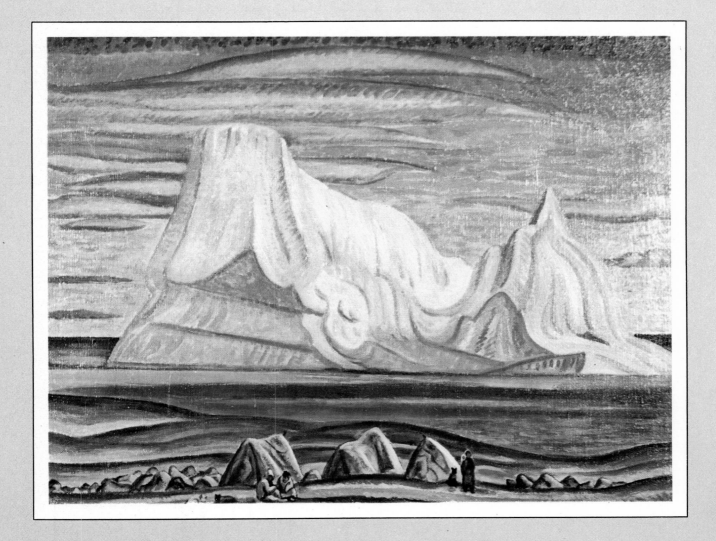

*This majestic berg was seen and swiftly sketched by
Jackson somewhere in north Baffin Bay on his second voyage to the high North. Art collector Charles Band bought
the painting in Toronto's "Greenwich Village" in 1930
at the urging of Group of Seven member, Arthur Lismer.*

"Exciting shapes on ancient Baffin: mountain, glacier, snow. The pervading colour of the rocks was a sort of violet-grey, a mauve."

Mount Asgard, and its glacier: The artist completed this canvas after his most recent Arctic visit. "When I was in Pangnirtung," he said, "an old Eskimo came up to me and said, 'I remember you — you came up here 35 years ago.'" At Frobisher, Jackson noted some Eskimos had autos now.

"The Alaska Highway, in the crisp October weather with the low sun, ice at the edge of the rivers . . . we found it fascinating."

In World War II, with permissions from Ottawa and Washington, Jackson and H. G. Glyde went on a painting safari on Alaska Highway. West of Whitehorse, near Kluane Lake, Jackson found this scene where "mile after mile of sharp peaks form the background to the lands of little sticks."

"Sixty miles south of the Coppermine settlement on the Arctic Ocean – a lovely country to walk over . . . with moss thick like a carpet."

By private plane from Yellowknife, A. Y. Jackson in 1949 made one of many trips above the Arctic Circle. A film about his work had made him a familiar figure, even in the N.W.T. "Sure I know who that old fellow is," said an Indian at Bear River, "I saw him in a movie at Norman Wells."

"At Canada's most northerly post, I made a quick sketch of the Beothic anchored a quarter of a mile from shore... the ice was closing in fast."

This painting, finished in 1928 after Jackson's first voyage to the R.C.M.P. post on Bache Peninsula, Ellesmere Island (with Dr. Banting), hangs in the National Gallery. On a later visit, ice prevented the ship from reaching the post and "we took a shaking up in a sea like a bucking broncho."

INDEX

127

PICTURE CREDITS

Order of appearance in the text of pictures listed here is left to right, top to bottom. After the first recording, principal sources are credited under these abbreviations:

Cover/John de Visser
1/Doug Wilkinson
2-3/Alan Collier
4/Ray Webber
4-5/Roloff Beny
7/Toronto Public Libraries
8-9/George Hunter
10/Farley Mowat
11-13/FM
14/National Film Board from Pierre Berton collection; NFB
15/Dept. of Energy, Mines and Resources
16/JDV
17/FM
18/JDV
19/FM
20-21/DW
23/TPL
24/Richard Harrington; DEMR; RH; RW
25/NFB; NFB
26-27/TPL
29/West-Baffin Eskimo Co-operative
30/Glenbow Foundation
31/TPL from a painting by Hon. John Collier; TPL
32/John Ross Robertson

Barley, Skagway Photo from Roy Minter Collection, RMC;
Roloff Beny, RB;
Pierre Berton Collection, PB;
Canadian Illustrated News, CIN;
Alan Collier, AC;
W. V. Crich, WVC;
Department of Energy, Mines & Resources, DEMR;

Collection, TPL
33/GF
34/Canadian Illustrated News; CIN
35/The Illustrated London News
36/National Gallery of Canada; TPL
37/DW
38/RW; RW; Pierre Berton Collection
39/DW; DW; PB
40/Hudson's Bay Company; Notman Photographic Archives; PB; NFB
41/JDV; DW
42/Thomas E. Lee
43/TEL; TEL
45-48/TPL
49/Public Archives of Canada
51-52/TPL
53/University of Toronto Library
54-56/TPL
57/George Eastman House
58-59/TPL
60-61/Ernest Brown Collection; Geological Survey of Canada
62/GF; Ralph Hedlin

John de Visser, JDV;
National Film Board, NFB;
Glenbow Foundation, GF;
C. G. Hampson, CGH;
David Hancock, DH;
Richard Harrington, RH;
George Hunter, GH;
A. Y. Jackson, AYJ;
Thomas E. Lee, TEL;
Farley Mowat, FM;

63/GF
64/Barley, Skagway Photo from Roy Minter Collection; Ernest Brown Collection (Alberta Govt. Photograph)
65-67/RMC
68-69/RMC
68/PB
69/Miller Services; Miller Services
70/National Aviation Museum; C. H. Dickens; National Aviation Museum
71/PB
73-75/WBEC
76/NFB
78/Povungnituk Cooperative Society
79/PCS; PCS
81-82/TPL
83/GF
84-86/TPL
87/David Hancock
88/Robert A. Ruttan
89/DH
90/DW; RB; DH; Walter Petrigo; DH; S. D. MacDonald, National Museum of Canada; SDM; SDM; J. C. Holroyd,

S. D. Macdonald, National Museum of Canada, SDM;
Povungnituk Cooperative Society, PCS;
James H. Soper, JHS;
Toronto Public Libraries, TPL;
West-Baffin Eskimo Co-operative, WBEC;
Webber, Ray, RW;

National Museum of Canada
91/W. V. Crich
92/WVC; DH; DH; WVC; DH; DH; WVC
92-93/C. G. Hampson; RB
94/George W. Scotter; TEL; James H. Soper; George W. Scotter; CGH; CGH; JHS; JHS; DH
95/JHS; CGH; JHS; CGH; CGH; CGH; JHS; JHS; CGH
97-100/TPL
101/CIN
103/Imperial Oil Collection
104/Imperial Oil Collection
109/Imperial Oil Collection
111-113/TPL
114-115/AC
118-119/Chico Slongo, Iron Ore Co. of Canada
120/Mrs. R. E. Dowsett Collection
121/Mrs. Charles Band Collection
122/Hudson's Bay Company Collection
123-125/National Gallery of Canada, Ottawa

ACKNOWLEDGEMENTS   A. Y. Jackson's paintings were photographed by Dennis Colwell and John Evans. Maps by W. G. Parlane.

For their assistance in reading the manuscript, the author thanks Dr. David A. Munro, Director, Canadian Wildlife Service, Department of Indian Affairs and Northern Development, Ottawa, and Mr. Alan Cooke, Centre d'Etudes Nordiques, Université Laval, Québec.

CREDITS   The type-faces chosen for this book are Juliana and Optima, set in Canada by Hunter Rose Co. Ltd. and Lino-Comp. The book was printed and bound in Italy by Arnoldo Mondadori, Officine Grafiche.

THE AUTHOR   Farley Mowat, winner of two Governor-General's Awards, is the best-known (and most outspoken) writer on the Canadian Arctic. His many books — including the best-selling *People of the Deer* — reflect his passionate concern for the welfare of the native peoples of the North.